Essays

An Analysis of Traditional and Marginal Literature

By S.R. Stewart

Copyright©2018 S.R. Stewart
All Rights Reserved
Published by Unsolicited Press in collaboration with *If You Give a Girl Media*.

No part of this book may be reproduced or transmitted in any form or by any means without written permission from the publisher or author.
Unsolicited Press Books are distributed by Ingram.
Printed in the United States of America.
Editor: Sophia Noulas

Attention schools and businesses: for discounted copies on large orders, please contact the publisher directly.

All proceeds of this novel are used to help children in American become more literate.

ISBN: 978-1-947021-59-4

To teachers who refuse to teach the syllabus. You are my inspiration.

Contents

Introduction

On Plays

2 Sarah Kane's *Blasted:* Sexual Violence and Disarming Nationalism

7 Edgar and Edmund: Fortune's View on Legitimacy

15 An Analysis—Death of a Salesman. 15

On Poetry

20 *Beowulf*: Roles of Women

27 Susan Howe's *That This*: Fallibility, Coping, and the Impact of Archives

55 Seamus Heaney's "Bog Queen": Ireland's Resistance to Historical Prejudice

63 The Dream Songs: Double-Talk and Sexual Repression in Society during the 1950s and 1960s

80 Fragmented Voices of a Whole

93 Eliot's Thwarted Lovers: An Allusion to Tristan and Isolde

96 Wordsworth and Whitman: Awakening of Selfhood in Silence

106 Shifting Values of Courtesy: "Sir Gawain and the Green Knight"

119 Male Control stripped by Female Identity

126 Explication Anne Finch's "Adam Pos'd"

129 Fame and Fortune, Lives' Forgotten: Thomas Gray's "Elegy Written in a Country Churchyard

137 Gwendolyn Brooks' "The Mother": Maternal Ambivalence and Agency in Non-Traditional Mothers

145 On CA Conrad's "How the Fuck Do I Get Out of this Place"

149 The New Boys

154 Cole Swensen's Gravesend

158 Harryette Mullen's S*p*rm**k*t

162 Claudia Rankine's Citizen

167 Charles Bernstein's Recalculating

171 Hello, the Roses

On Prose

176 Wolf-Alice: Mirrors, Menstruation, and Language

189 *Pride and Prejudice*: Propriety and Moderation

200 *Their Eyes Were Watching God*: Intersectionality of the Mule and Janie's Hair and How Janie's Claims Her Identity

212 Fosdick: The Foil of *Ragged Dick* and the Highlighted Values of Industrial Capitalism

222 A New England Nun: Unconventional Sexuality and Autonomy

235 *The Female American*: Marginalized Identity Transcends Patriarchy

246 Thoughts on Captivity Narratives

249 Maternal Inheritance in *Breath, Eyes, Memory*

253 The Disruption of Filial Piety in *Charlotte Temple*

On Philosophy and History

264 Role of Virginity and Independence of Women in Classical Athens Depicted in the Goddesses: Artemis, Athena, and Aphrodite

277 Knowledge in sixteenth/seventeenth Century Europe: A Departure from Aristotelian Scholasticism to Rationalism Based on the Authorities of Religion, Experience, and Reason

292 The Visions of European Unity

302 Stress during WWII

311 As a Whole: The Intersection of Brooks and Moretti

321 Six Degrees of Thingness: Or Just a Pun on Words.

333 Works Cited

Introduction

My college education was superb. I received a B.A. in English from U.C. Davis and thanks to those brave professors, I hardly encountered the canonical works of Shelley or Fitzgerald, not to say that they aren't great writers...but come on, there are better ones. I am not saying those books aren't worth the read, but plenty of other marginalized authors and books are just as important to literature.

I set off to curate this group of essays from my undergraduate days because I wanted to show what a body of work looked like from a writer and scholar who was hardly exposed to major writers. Yes, I read John Berryman and I was asked to read *Pride and Prejudice*, but never was I asked to look at these books through a traditional literary lens. Many of the classes I took on literature were skewed through a queer or obscure lens. Famous and marginalized literature was examined in terms of a mother's role or a Native American's role. For that, I am forever grateful to the professors at my alma mater. Without them, I would have missed out on a different way to think about books – about our world through literature.

While an introduction isn't usually the place for a thank you to friends, I am going to do it anyways. I want to say thank you to Unsolicited Press for being the best damn company to work for – I especially want to thank my sister-in-crime, Rubie, for her support and incessant desire to promote my work. Of course, thank you friends. Family.

On Plays

Sarah Kane's *Blasted:* Sexual Violence and Disarming Nationalism

In Sarah Kane's play *Blasted*, sexual violence highlights and disarms the negative implications of nationalism. How? Through the characterization of Ian, a journalist, and the soldier who invades. Isolation and elitist perspectives are the negative repercussions of nationalism discussed in Kane's treatment of war. Ian's characterizations before and after the sexual assault show the impacts of nationalism, and its destruction.

At the beginning of the play, Ian portrays a strong Englishman who wields his gun and uses racial slurs to prove his elitist attitude, however, after he is sexual assaulted; he does not keep the same nationalistic perspective. For example, in Scene 1, Ian says, "I've shat in better places that this," and "Hate this city. Stinks. Wogs and Pakis taking over," (Kane 4). Ian's sense of nationalism is expressed through his character to reveal an elitist perspective on the ethnic population in Leeds. Moreover, prior to the sexual assault by Soldier, Ian is adamant to declare, "I'm Welsh," and "I'm not an import," in response to Soldier asking him if he was fighting for the same cause (41). The ideology of "un-English (or Welsh)" has seriously influenced the way Ian views others in society, whether living in Leeds or elsewhere.

After Soldier, a man who is neither English nor Welsh, rapes Ian, his elitist identity is disarmed and Ian becomes like others in the face of conflict. For example, Soldier tells Ian, "Don't think your Welsh arse is different to any other arse I fucked" (50). Considering that, this sexual act was identical to that of Soldier's girlfriend; Ian's sense of nationalism is removed because he was subjected to an experience that many other nationalities have experienced too. Kane shows that Ian's nationalistic attitude is neutralized with the stage direction, "He is hugging the Soldier's body for comfort," which highlights that at the most primal level, communal humanity exists outside of the pitfalls of nationalism (60). Ian forgoes his elitist perspective to fulfill his most basic human needs: to be in the presence of another person and to be comforted in a time of need. Through the sexual violence, Kane highlights that the impact of a national identity (which causes the very conflict that Ian endures) can be dismantled to allow cosmopolitanism to surface on the face of violence.

In relation to Ian's character exhibiting the negative implications of nationalism and its destruction, the characterization of Soldier further argues that nationalism's negative implications can disrupt a worldwide community. Yet, Kane disarms Soldier's nationalistic predation in the latter end of the play. Soldier enters the play at the end of Scene Two with an empowered attitude, as he removes Ian's gun and orders him around. The soldier raping Ian and recounting his other violent sexual assaults demonstrates the side effects of strong nationalistic views. For example, in Scene Three Soldier tells Ian, "Our town now," implying that Ian's nationality is now beneath the nationality of those that have invaded the area (39). Afterward, Soldier rapes Ian, an act that physically puts his "nationality" inside Ian to show that nationalism creates unhealthy elitist attitudes (and competition) toward those who are not the same nationality. Not only does the rape render Ian's nationalistic identity worthless, it reveals that Soldier is creating a new elitist attitude for his own nationality. Furthermore, Soldier recounts a "young girl [he] fucked hand up inside her trying to claw [his] liquid out" which highlights the concept of maintaining a pure nationality (50). The soldier raped the girl to establish national dominance yet also used his power to avoid the conception of an impure child because of his need to force his nationalism on an innocent girl. At last, Kane uses Soldier to rectify the discrimination that results from nationalism through the intimate act that occurs between Ian and Soldier after the rape. The stage direction shows, "He [Soldier] puts his mouth over one of Ian's eyes, sucks it out, bites it off and eats it" (50). Soldier blinds Ian to the implications of an elitist national identity by physically disabling Ian's ability to judge a person's exterior. It would seem as though Kane is making an argument that the sexual violence, regardless of the horrific nature, disarms nationalism and allows humanity to thrive without borders.

Edgar and Edmund: Fortune's View on Legitimacy

The themes of legitimacy and fortune are interwoven throughout William Shakespeare's *King Lear*. The prevalence leads one to ask, "Is legitimacy leading the actions or is fortune and integrity determining one's legitimacy, thereby the actions, too?" Shakespeare explores this question wildly in his darkest. For clarity, the terms legitimacy and (wheel of) fortune need to be defined. Legitimacy is the legal status of one's birth. A person born in wedlock is legitimate, while a person born out of wedlock is illegitimate. Additionally, the wheel of fortune is a cycle of fate that propels people to the top and to the bottom of the wheel. The wheel is constantly propelling the fates of the characters within the premise of *King Lear*. Gloucester's sons, the illegitimate Edmund and the legitimate Edgar are affected by the interwoven themes of legitimacy and fortune. Moreover, the idea of what is legitimate is viewed as an inborn characteristic. However, Shakespeare implies that the wheel of fortune, alongside one's perceived integrity, controls one's legitimacy status. Edmund and Edgar's status changes as the wheel of fortune turns or their perceived integrity changes (both products of fate). Whilst it is common to consider legitimacy as an innate property, Edmund and Edgar in Shakespeare's *King Lear* demonstrate that perceived integrity and the wheel of fortune govern legitimacy.

The legitimacy status of Edmund and Edgar is not concrete; rather, it can be altered through one's perceived integrity. Two passages in *King Lear* highlight this process: the first is during Edmund's plot against Edgar and the second is at the close of the play when Edmund's plot is exposed to the court. First, in Act 1, Scene 2, Edmund plots against Edgar, saying,

"Legitimate Edgar, I must have your land.
Our father's love is to Edmund.
As to the legitimate. Fine word-legitimate"!
Well, my legitimate, if this letter speed,
And my invention thrive. Edmund the base shall top the legitimate…"

Edmund claims that he will defame Edgar's integrity to make his own integrity shine (1.2.16–21). Thus, Edmund will be considered the more legitimate son and be entitled to the public arena that Edgar is currently entitled to. He is successful in his quest to turn Edgar into the illegitimate bastard. Gloucester, their father is fooled by Edmund's plot and states, "unnatural detested, brutish villain!" in regard to his son Edgar (1.2.77). Gloucester views Edgar's integrity as tarnished, thereby turning him into the unnatural and illegitimate son. This grants Edmund the place of the legitimate, as his integrity seems intact. Also, Edmund's newfound integrity and legal status propel him to the top with the noble men. For example, in Act 3, Scene 5, Edmund uses his perceived integrity to win the heart of Cornwall. Cornwall says, "it hath made thee Earl of Gloucester" in response to Edmund citing that his "malicious fortune" had given him traitors in his family (3.5.15–16). Cornwall says, "thou shalt find a dearer father in my love" granting Edmund the status as a legitimate son too (3.5.22–23). Here, legitimacy by birth is not permanent; it is directly influenced by one's perceived integrity. The higher the integrity one is perceived to possess, the more legitimate one becomes.

Anthony Daniels of The New Criterion agrees that one's legitimacy status is not inborn, but it is something that the characters in *King Lear* can manipulate through perception and deception. Daniels states, "human conduct [with regards to Edmund's plot] has been turned to advantage by one who held it, or appeared to hold it, and indeed it could be said [that the characteristics] have been founded upon little else" (Daniels, 9). Additionally, Shakespeare hints that legitimacy is not the marker that creates action and the people within the action, thus this evidence further bolsters the theme of legitimacy being affected by others' perceptions of Edmund and Edgar. Furthermore, at the end of the play in Act 5, Scene 3, Edgar implies that Edmund is a traitor and a deceiver of the court. At this point, Edmund is unaware that the disguised man is Edgar, thus Edmund claims, "But what art thou that hast this fortune one me? If thou'rt noble, I do forgive thee" (5.3.164–166). Thus, Edmund will confess if the person placing these charges of deception against is of a nobler status. One's legitimacy seems to run how the action is played out in this play. Edgar reveals himself to the court and forces Edmund to confess to his crimes. Edmund sinks back into the illegitimate position, while Edgar regains his status as the legitimate son. In this case, Edmund lost his integrity to Edgar, thereby regaining the status as an illegitimate son.

Additionally, Edmund and Edgar's legitimacy changes as the wheel of fortune is called upon to turn. The wheel of fortune turns itself, placing one person at the height of fortune and one at its counterpoint. It seems in *King Lear* that fortune has it hands on the character's legitimacy status. For example, Edmund states, "I grow. I prosper." When he invokes the wheel of fortune to churn him to the top of the wheel and allow his plot to be successful (1.2.129). At the top of the wheel, Edmund becomes the legitimate son, inheriting all of Edgar's rights to land and status, while Edgar is cast out as a criminal with zero status in the court. Moreover, Edmund beckons "briefness and fortune work," after he begins to see the profit of being the legitimate son. Fortune aids Edmund into becoming the legitimate son, while turning Edgar into the illegitimate son. A dark undertone resonates in Edmund believing that he can call on fortune to alter his legitimacy. It is as though he believes that he can control his fate and legitimacy through the wheel of fortune. Frances Biscoglio of *The Shakespeare Newsletter* agrees, stating that "the individual controls the forces of the universe and manipulate them to serve human desires" (Biscoglio 2001). Edmund believes the he changes his legitimacy through a manipulation of Fortune, thereby granting him the wishes that he desires. However, this is the discord that Shakespeare points out: humans cannot demand fortune to obey them, rather the cycle of fortune and one's fate control all aspects of humans, including legitimacy. This is witnessed at the end of the play when the wheel of fortune completes its cycle and Edmund returns to being the illegitimate son and Edgar is welcomed back into the court as a man with noble status. Edmund states, "Thou has spoken right 'tis true. The wheel is come full circle. I am here." (5.3.173–175). Fortune cannot be controlled; rather it controls all actions and status of the people in King Lear's court. Moreover, fortune turned Edmund back into an illegitimate son demonstrating that legitimacy is not an innate characteristic, but it is a social marker that can be adjusted to the circumstances. Joseph Alulis, author of "Wisdom and Fortune: The Education of the Prince in Shakespeare's *King Lear*," states that "people do seem to get away with the natural law," and "fortune only touches external things," to imply that legitimacy is something that can be broken or changed by fate and fortune (Alulis, 2010). He is correct. In the play, it seems that legitimacy is a label of the natural law that can be manipulate by fortune or the characters within the plot.

  The themes in Shakespeare's King Lear draw on the darkest qualities of humanity and society. It exploits the silliness of labeling persons as legitimate or illegitimate based on the way in which they were born into this world. Legitimacy is not an inborn quality; rather a person can be illegitimate based on their actions, perceived actions, or by the cards of fate. Shakespeare proves that legitimacy is not innate by demonstrating that Edmund had the ability to change his outward status of illegitimate through the use of deception. He manipulated others into believing that his integrity was of a richer sort than his legitimate brother Edgar's integrity. Edgar fell prey to the quickness of his society to believe that he would plot against his father. Moreover, legitimacy is shown to be at the hands of fortune's wheel. As the wheel of fortune turned to bring Edmund to the height of the wheel and legitimate, it brought him back down to the illegitimate position, as well. Legitimacy changes constantly, thus, it is not possible for it to be a permanent property of the characters in *King Lear*.

An Analysis—Death of a Salesman

Death of a Salesman by Arthur Miller provides a great set of intriguing characters; Biff Loman is the perfect example of a person filled with the struggle to be good and overcome his negative desires. Biff is a man who feels lost, is losing his father to dementia, and is realizing everything he learned as a child was a lie. He struggles to discover the truth and expose the lies that his family has created even if it tears them apart. Biff possesses many negative and positive characteristics, while the suffering of his father is what makes him become a man.

Throughout Biff's life he has been a kleptomaniac, which is the negative quality that led him to his epiphany. Biff steals to defy authority until the end of his father's life. As a young boy, Biff happily stole lumber from the nearby construction to make his father happy. Young Bernard runs to Willy, his father, and states, "the watchman's chasing Biff" and Willy does not do a thing (802). Biff learns that he can be careless toward authority, so the reason he has not made a career for himself. He realizes that he steals to get what he cannot have, due to the pressure of his father. When Biff steals the fountain pen from Bill Oliver in Act 2, Biff stops in the stairs and cries, "And I looked at the pen and said to myself, what the hell am I grabbing this pen for?" (833). He did not want the pen, he wanted the life his father turned down, which was to work on a ranch in the West. The pen symbolized the career that he did not have, and at this point he saw that he had to make a change in his life. Biff decides to return the pen and make things right with his family. He becomes humble and sees that stealing had nothing to do with authority, but it had everything to do with being something he was not.

 Everyone led Biff to believe that he was the best at everything that he did not have to work to be great which became his major downfall, but later teaching him that the world does not work that way. Since childhood, Biff's stardom made his father think that he did not have to try to succeed;

the school would not flunk him since Willy told him he was so great in Act One. Biff believed that, and it came as a shock when he failed (780). However, that was not the only reason. The discovery of his father's affair forced Biff to lose hope in himself to achieve the American Dream. Willy's affair opened the world of lies up to Biff, and he did not want to turn out the same way; Biff wanted to avoid being unhappy like his father. At Biff's wits ends at the close of Act Two, he cries to Willy that "I'm not bringing any prizes anymore."(834) He shattered the false reality that his family had created to start a better life.

    The shock of the lies made Biff's morals step into gear and turn away from the negative aspects of his life. Biff is protective of his mother and tries to shelter her from the truth of his father's adultery. This positive quality allows the reader to view Biff from a different perspective. Most of the play focuses on Biff's faults, but this is something nobody can deny. He is all about his family and will do anything to save them. From the start Biff tells his father not to talk to his mother that way and continues that attitude until his father's death.

In the end, Biff became more of a man than his father could ever make him. He learned that being a kleptomaniac was a result of his resentment toward his father for not letting him live out his dream. On top of that, the struggle he went through to find a job to please his family proves that while he may not be a good guy, he is trying to succeed without it just falling into his lap. Miller portrays a character who has much to learn, but can break away from his family's lies and become the man that he wants to be. Biff's character shows the struggle for the American Dream.

On Poetry

Beowulf: Roles of Women

Throughout the history of literature, female characters are often peripheral characters that do not get much recognition from readers. Further analysis of male-centric works, reveals that women play central roles in literature regardless of the proximity to the protagonist who is struggling with internal and external conflicts. Many of these conflicts in literature lead to significant analysis of the moral fabric that defines such a character. For example, the epic of *Beowulf* is revered for its accounts of heroism and male comradery. Beowulf is a courageous hero who defeats three monsters for the sake of a nearby country. The women in Beowulf are overlooked, however, a close examination of the poetry demonstrates that the women play roles that are central to the story and to that of society. Three major women play integral roles throughout the epic: Wealhtheow, Grendel's Mother, and Hildeburh. These women entertain, bring peace, and contradict societal expectations of the female gender, either directly or indirectly. Women fall into these roles because the male-dominated society does not allow for women to venture out into other archetypes. The roles of the hostess and the peacemaker are inherent to the conditioned female nature, while the monster is the unmodified female in her natural state of being. The epic of "Beowulf" illustrates three major roles for women in the society: the peacemaker, the hostess, and the monster.

  The peacemaker is a low powered, yet pivotal role played by the women throughout the epic of *Beowulf*. As a peacemaker, the woman is responsible for uniting tribes (warring or not) and maintaining solid relations between these groups. The strongest model of the peacemaker in *Beowulf*, is Hildeburh, the Danish princess who was married off to the King of Jutes. Hildeburh is a gift from the Danes to the Jutes in hopes to bring peace between the countries and establish an alliance. Author Nicole Smith of the *Journal of Medieval History* claims that Hildeburh's main job as a "happily confined" queen is to act as a "mediator and a departure from male-dominated activities and relationships," which means that she eases tensions that may arise between men. Furthermore, when Hildeburh's brother of Danes and son of Jutes perish in a battle in which they are enemies, she stresses that they be burned together (*Beowulf*, ll. 1070–1185). Her desire to burn enemies together demonstrates an act of joining the opposed forces regardless of the alliances. Although the marriage did not bring peace to these groups of people, Hildeburh fulfilled her duty as a peacemaker by maintaining loyalties with her homeland and the land of her husband.

In addition to the peacemaker, the queen in *Beowulf* acts as hostess to the men of the land. It is important to note that the hostess does not solely serve the men, rather she is the instrument that reaffirms social customs and publicly establishes the status of the men who are in the presence of the king. Wealhtheow, the queen of Daneland and wife of Hrothgar completes these duties in the mead hall when the warriors are dining with the king. For example, Wealhtheow establishes a warrior's status by using the cup of mead. She carries the cup of mead starting with the king and then to the warriors. In the first scene, she serves Beowulf last since he had just arrived in Daneland. However, in lines 1162–1231, she serves Beowulf directly after serving her husband. The act of the cup demonstrates that Beowulf has earned his right to sit beside the king, as though he were a Dane himself (Porter, 1).

      Furthermore, the hostess holds political power in the hall. Wealhtheow demonstrates this power by publicly requesting that the King not allow Beowulf to be the heir to the throne, but to remember that her sons are the rightful heirs to such a position (*Beowulf*, ll. 1180–1191). She is confident that the King will abide by these social customs and there is no reprimand or indication in the poem that her wishes will not be granted (Porter, 1). Beowulf does become the king; however, he only holds the place until the sons are old enough to fulfill their duty as king. The hostess becomes the voice of reason; she is responsible for upholding the social customs of her country when all the warriors have forgotten the importance of these codes.

Unlike the peacemaker and the hostess, the female monster embodies masculine energy and acts contrary to the social expectations of a woman in society. The most important female monster in *Beowulf* is Grendel's mother. First, the female monster uses physical force and violence to solve conflict. For example, Grendel's mother attacks anyone that enters her cave without reason (*Beowulf*, ll. 1259–1260). Grendel's mother is a "hostile hostess" who uses "the sword to rid her hall . . . of unwanted hall guests" (Porter, 2). The behavior Grendel's mother exhibits is masculine and demonstrates that the female monster does not solve conflict with words and marriage (like the peacemakers and hostesses), but with physical action. This masculine behavior per the poet should never be tolerated regardless of social status (*Beowulf*, ll 1940–1943). Moreover, the female monster exhibits unexpected masculine energy by engaging in the customs assigned to a warrior. In this society, only men seek vengeance, therefore a woman that does so is considered villainous for disobeying the expected behavior of a female in civilized society. After the death of her son, Grendel's mother goes on a "sorrowful journey to avenge her slain son" (*Beowulf*, lines 1276–78). Smith claims that "her role as an avenger" makes her disturbing and "grotesque" for her ability "to carry out the male-dominated act of revenge." Seeking vengeance is not acceptable as a female. Her actions make her an outcast, a monster to the village because she does not fulfill her female duties. These qualities in a woman during this time classify her as a monster.

The epic of *Beowulf* is lined with heroic men seeking vengeance, ruling halls, and fighting battles. The women in the story are expected to fulfill duties that best serve the men of the land. The importance of the roles that women adopt in the story are underestimated. Many of the women have more power than one would expect during this time. The roles are central to the story and in maintaining a civilized society. The peacemaker weaves herself between lands to form alliances, while the hostess serves as a political instrument that brings hospitality and order to the land. At last, the monster is a complex character that opposes the social expectations of a female and utilizes the law of man to solve problems. Although the poet does not exalt the women in the story for their influence over men, the role of women should be considered to fully grasp the purpose of the actions taken throughout the epic.

Susan Howe's *That This*: Fallibility, Coping, and the Impact of Archives

When a loved one passes, nothing is left but physical belongings to be curated into an archive that represents the former identity. That identity is shaped by the person, persons, or entity responsible for selecting the relics, and as a result is not an accurate representation of the past. Despite that discrepancy, archives play a crucial role in our understanding of history. Archives offer an emotional, physical, and metaphysical connection between the past and the present. For those closest to the deceased (in time and by relationship), these physical objects are more than just physical relics; these objects allow an engagement between the living and the dead—even a spiritual tether—that functions as a way to cope with death and as a way to understand humanity. In a world where afterlife is uncertain, those who engage with archives keep the past actively living within the present. Susan Howe's *That This* is a grappling with archives as the speaker (admittedly Susan Howe) copes with her husband's passing. She navigates her grief by encountering her husband's belongings and in her examination of the Edwards' family belongings that have been archived in several libraries. The collection is split into three sections: "The Disappearance Approach," "Frolic Architecture," and "That This." Because of the unique nature of Howe's collection, with the "I" admittedly being the poet, it is important to note that I use Howe's name and "the speaker" interchangeably. Through form, tone, diction, and figurative language, Howe's collection points out the impact of the archival on the present, especially when considering the intimate relationships between the living and lost loved ones. The collection shows the fallibility of the archival, and its inability to accurately represent the past since the past is mediated by the living. The past can never be represented in truth. While that fallibility is disruptive toward preserving an accurate account of history, Howe shows that the lingering emotional connection between relics and the living may be just as important as people seek to make sense of the past and its ability to inform the present.

The archive of a loved one's belongings has territorial ties that both draw the speaker into the past and push her away, treating her like an intruder. In Howe's case, she always wants to be let in, as her obsession with the past, regardless of whose past it is, intoxicates her and impacts her decisions to move forward with her relationship. For example, Howe recounts her late-husband's home prior to marriage upon his request for her to move in with him; she notes that the decision was not simple because "it was the first wife's territory" and she clearly did not "share her taste" in home décor (16). The lingering style aesthetics demonstrate that her husband was unable to fully rid the home of his late-wife, but more importantly, it positioned Howe as an outsider. Her wavering, however, does not last long, as she is drawn into the home by "old family oil portraits, various objects from the China Trade, engravings of genteel nineteenth-century Episcopalian ministers" (16). The rich history of Peter's past has control over

her—the desire to connect with history—
and results in her decision to move in with
him. Howe's urge to surround herself with
the relics is not solely from a historian-
academic desire, but it is a demand that "the
archive itself must not only be understood,
but encountered" by the speaker on an
emotional, physical, and metaphysical plane
(West, 628). The encounter with the archive
allows the past to persist into the present;
Howe's engagement gives the past life.

Does this engagement result in the
speaker's having diminished agency? Or is it
her agency that permits her to converse and
connect with the physical remnants of the
past? The first section "The Disappearance
Approach" suggests a bit of both in Howe,
although free will may be confused with
curiosity. A stronger argument could be
made that the past has a strong hold over the
speaker, prior to her husband's passing and
afterwards. For example, revisiting the
passage in which Howe describes her
husband's familial relics and her decision to
move in with him, the speaker states that the
belongings "beckoned me into an
environment where ancestors figured as

tender grass springing out of the earth" (17). Howe plays with language here, metaphorically and through personification, and both serve to play to Howe's weakness for the past. First, the relics are personified, beckoning the speaker into the home; she is summoned into the home to engage with the past. According to the *Oxford English Dictionary*, "beckon" means to make a significant, mute gesture with a finger, head, or hand. The items are ushering her into the home where the dead have agency and voice through objects (of course, only a representative one). The metaphor of freshly sprung grass argues that the ancestors are reborn upon Howe's decision to step into the home permanently. Howe's agency is not diminished; rather, it is her agency that allows the relics to come to life. In this, Howe grants them agency and as West points out, "Howe discovers and rescues from the archive, voices silent and silenced" (617). Ultimately, I see the relationship as a mutual one: the archive needs Howe to resurrect the voices of the past and give them a voice in the present, while Howe needs to encounter the relics to keep the tether between the present and the past in order to cope with the loss of her loved ones. The relationship is symbiotic with the relics and Howe having agency, but Howe has more agency as she is the one who makes the decision to encounter the relics. Her inquisitive curiosity with silenced voices and their relationship to the present moves beyond an intellectual journey; the engagement with remnants of her husband and of the Edwards family help her navigate the loss of her husband, keeping the conversation between them from dying.

The tone of Howe in "The Disappearance Approach" is inquisitive of the purpose of holding onto the physical objects of loved ones as she navigates her husband Peter's death and perhaps understanding why archives can become so important in the maintenance of identity of past and present. Since it is understood that loved ones cannot return as they once were, the connection must be preserved with a connection between the living and physical representations of those who once were. Howe argues that perhaps this relationship is "some not yet understood return to people we have loved and lost" (17). She seeks the reason the identity of the living becomes hinged on the former identities of the dead. Her tone while inquisitive is also hollow as she continues on to say, "I need to imagine the possibility even if I don't believe it" (17). Emotionally, the speaker feels the need to surround herself (and engage) with her husband's things, but the pragmatist in her peeks outs, showing the reader Howe's stance on existence and otherworld potential. The struggle to cope with Peter's death sparks a new reason to engage with archives; the engagement becomes fiercely personal. Her connection to archives becomes deeper; she becomes an active participant in the rebirth of the dead. And this personal connection to her husband's things spills over into her obsession with other family's archives. In an interview with *The Paris Review*, Howe says "there's still a bodily trace" in the things left behind and that tether "is all we have to connect with the dead" (McLane). Physical remnants contain a trace or a thread that the living clings to and that the living uses to reinvigorate the past. By keeping the past and the present in conversation with one another, identity is preserved.

Beyond that, the notion of traces appears several times in "The Disappearance Approach" as the driving force of the connection between the past and the present, between the speaker and the dead. As Howe interacts with her late-husband's belongings, she feels the pressure of the dead pressing upon her, saying there is "an intense impression of the past pressing heavily on the present, I often feel when I'm alone with his books and papers" (18). The heavy use of alliteration in this statement gives physical weight to the past as the speaker engages with Peter's things. Additionally, the words "intense" and "pressing" carry strength too. It is as if the spirit, or the trace of Peter bears weight upon the speaker. And while Howe has admitted to the reader that she does not believe in the afterlife of spirits, it is clear that the speaker senses the traces of the past coming through the physical objects. The relationship is immensely intimate, serving as a way for the living to grieve and cope with death, while forming a tangible connection with the intangible. Archives are the medium for conversation with the "echoes of life arriving telepathically from past to present at the instant of discovery" as the speaker encounters the past within the remnants circulating in the present. The connection with archives forms the identity of the past and the present.

Howe's strongest connection to the past comes when she encounters the "written traces" in the writings, books, and papers of the dead (importantly her husband and in her exploration of the Edwards' family remnants). The trace, and the pressure of the past becomes most apparent when Howe enters Peter's study, a room her late husband "rarely used…except as a strange space for his many books" (18). Inside the study is a "dilapidated desk" built by Peter's father that is "littered with old syllabi, letters, and journals" (18). First, the use of the term dilapidated grabs my attention because it defines that desk as decaying and, because it houses old remnants kept by Peter, it seems to function as an unorganized vault for his yet-to-be archived materials. Not to mention, it links the present further to the past since the desk was built by his father, thus showing the process of passing historical relics from one generation to the next. More importantly, the choice of items collected by Peter and listed by Howe is significant because it not only demonstrates what the speaker finds as valuable remnants of her husband, but the list represents what Peter identified with as well. In life, Peter was a philosopher and professor. The old syllabi, which lose value after a class concludes, remained in his study, not because he needed them for later use, but because they made up a part of his identity as a scholar. Moreover, the letters, presumably received by friends, family, and scholars represent his social connections. And the journals, whether they were private writings or academic publications, further encompass who Peter believed himself to be in life. These items are the essence of Peter's identity for himself and for the speaker. Howe uses the relics to be with Peter and to keep her footing in reality, even if that reality is entirely subjective.

 An odd facet of this passage is the function of the study as an archive for

Peter's belongings before he passed away, as if he began curating his own archive in his lifetime. What does that say about the impact of objects on identity? On the preservation of self? Do we amass books, papers, and tokens that represent our own perceived identity long before death pulls us into "eternal wordlessness" (14)? Perhaps, and perhaps not. But what is known is that the archived materials must wait for the speaker to give them a voice and until that happens, they are merely objects without a trace of self.

What is clear for Howe is the impact particular writings have on informing her understanding of the past and the present, and what she thought she knew about reality and how she begins to understand that archives are little more than a subjective representation of what once was. The archived writings comfort and disturb her. For example, she is comforted because she witnesses a glimpse of Peter's interiority after he has died, but she is also disturbed because she realizes that it is "impossible to truly know another person" while alive or through the words and figures left behind

(Deming, *The Boston Review*). Howe can read Peter's writings and she can look at his books, but she can never fully access his identity. In her solitude of their once-shared home, Howe notes that "people disappear into never-answered questions" and all that remains are "echo-fragments" (28–29). The tone of the first statement is resolute. It is also terrifying to disappear into history with the only things remaining are materials to preserve the self through the interpretation of others. Likewise, to exist as fragmented echoes suggests that the former self is partially audible, with the remainder of the self to be filled in by those engaging with the tangible fragments of identity left behind in writings and relics. The speaker is left with questions of existence and of the fact that she can only ever know her husband based on her interpretation of the fragments. Did he ever exist? Does she exist? To cope with the disturbing thought that she never truly knew her husband, despite the strong connection she feels with Peter's things, she seeks to fill the "tremendous silence" that fills the house (19). To combat the silence, she looks to flowers, particularly

Paperwhites—one of Peter's favorite flowers—to "fill the room between [their] workspaces" (19). The loss of her husband becomes almost too much to bear, and the speaker feels the need to separate herself from the relics within the study that continue to remind her of the emptiness death brings. After all, the relics only have a voice when she provides it to them. Moreover, the use of Paperwhites is critical because these flowers often symbolize rebirth and renewal because it is typically one of the first flowers to bloom in the spring. Thus, the flowers represent sustained life that does not require an intermediary to bring it into the present. On the other hand, Peter's archives must "signal an attempt to express an intense interior life," but only through the subjectivity and engagement of the speaker (Deming). Although she wants to fill the silence, the collection does not suggest that she does it with anything other than archive materials and her obsession with the connection between the present and the past.

During her mourning and journey to engage with Peter through his books and papers, she recognizes that she will forever be "haunted by distance and disappearance" that is born out of death when she asks, "Do we ever know each other; know who we really are?" (34). The question of existence resurfaces as a means to understand the self and the other within time, but also to understand the function of archives. In "The Disappearance Approach," we discover that Howe's husband has been cremated, and so he has no gravestone. Howe states, "all I lack is your personal name on a tilted stone" in a moment of contemplation on proof of existence and the need for his name to be represented in the world (29). The word "lack" invites the reader to question proof of existence, and as Howe previously put it earlier in her collection, how are the living to know somebody has existed if we only "rely on written traces" (15)? Lack implies that although she knows he existed in her reality, the written proof is not there because there is not a stone with his name on it to say so. The word suggests that history, without physical objects to verify identity, erases the past. Howe is saying that "we exist in time, both in a historical and personal sense, and yet are left without the ability to fully grasp our individual relationships to time" (Herack, 434). The speaker knows her relationship to Peter. She knows that he lived and that his ashes are in the closet alongside his suit, but without the physical tethers between the past and the present, there is no way of knowing when. Time becomes an enemy to the past when archives are not in place. Moreover, the word "tilted" adds an air of oddness to the sentence. While some gravestones are tilted, most are erected upright. Here, the word tilted suggests that something is askew. What is askew? I would argue that the "tilted stone" stands in for the archives being unable to accurately represent the past.

Howe's collection reveals through her exploration of the Edwards family archive, that archives are fallible because they are subjective, mediated representations of the past. The past's identity is no more than a half-truth rearticulated by the living who encounter it. For example, Howe discusses the Edwards family, an 18th-century family with an extensive collection of written material housed by several organizations.

Howe informs the reader that the ten daughters "received the same education" and "were tutored along with their brother...in theology, philosophy, Latin, Greek, Hebrew, history, and mathematics" during a time when dedication to female education was rare (20–21). The women attended finishing school and married late in life with the exception of Mary who stayed behind to care for her grandparents and parents. And despite this accomplishment, Howe divulges that the "Beinecke Library in New Haven owns a vast collection of...letters, diaries, notebooks, essays and sermons," yet "all that remains of this 18th-century family's impressive tradition of female learning are a bedsheet...Sarah's wedding dress fragment, and several pages of Hannah Edwards Wetmore's private writings" (21). Moreover, the "Connecticut Historical Society in Hartford owns a fragment of Mary Edwards' crewel embroidery, and a pair of silk shoes" (21). These women's intellectual lives are hidden from view with the archive holding heavily to the sermons delivered by Jonathan Edwards. All that remains are the domestic tokens that would have been expected to be produced by women during this century. Their identities adjusted to fit the gendered expectations rather than provide an accurate account of their lives. And while one would expect a more violent tone from a speaker who relies heavily on the past to inform the present, a calm tone exists in the speaker's voice. The calm tone exists to keep a balanced approach, so as not to disturb the facts, and what surfaces from that calmness is Howe exposing the biased representation of this family's history. This is not the first time that Howe has sought to unbend gender bias in archives. In *My Emily Dickinson*, Howe examined Emily Dickinson's life and her poetry in a time that women were not expected to be poets. She discusses the fact that the "editing of her extraordinarily complex manuscripts has basically been in charge by two men" (McLane). While my focus within this essay is not gender bias, it is important to the argument that archives are built and skewed by individuals and authorities with various intentions. From the curation to the personal encounter with relics, an incredible amount of space exists for error in both the representation and extrapolation of meaning of the past. Howe, as a historian and poet, is concerned with the "opacities of personal and historical memory" of the archive (Nicholls, 441). It then makes sense that she would weave the Edwards family archive within the grieving process of her husband because it becomes clear to her that the past can be altered and shaped not only by those in charge of curating the archive, but of the people who choose to encounter it. She understands that subjectivity interferes with the ability to see the past in its whole and true form because the past is interpreted by the living (who hold various biases and emotional connections to different facets of the past). Thus, a half-true representation of the past informs the present.

    To correct the erroneous representation, Howe seeks to unsettle history as it is presented by making her own record of the Edwards family interspersed within her exposition on the loss of Peter. Howe interweaves the women's names and bits of their writing into her own writing as a way to rearticulate the past. She does not claim to do so with an unbiased authority either. During her accounts of Peter and the Edwards family, she says that compiling an account of the past is "putting bits of memory together, trying to pick out the good while doing away with the bad" (13). Howe's tone is understanding of erroneous facets of the archival and, in the death of her husband, she recognizes that the archival is an incredibly subjective account of the past. Memory is fallible. It is human nature for individuals to select the memories and the records of the past that fit into what is desired to be represented, even if that yields a false account of history. She knows that her understanding of history is personal and alterable when she says, "we never realize the full loyal one" (19). Here, "we" represents the individuals who can access archives; "we" represents the present. The phrase "full loyal one" is a distinctive personification of history because it argues that history that we can trust is never fully accessible. History is subjected to the needs of the living. The materials left behind by the deceased is subject to personal interpretations and emotional connections to the traces of what once was, but that changes depending on who is encountering the remnants. For the grieving speaker, the remnants of her husband help her manage the loss. On the other hand, for the speaker as historian-poet, the remnants may serve an entirely different purpose.

This comes back to the notion that a personal connection with history may be more important than knowing the whole truth, especially when the connection is an intimate piece of one's identity. Engagement with archives and seeking to find meaning within the past is integral to understanding the present and in Howe's case, managing her grief. Furthermore, Howe recognizes that engagement with the past is "modified by the one who looks into it and articulates it (Crown, 491). Looking into the past in search of meaning may allow for a "revision of ideas in the present," but with the understanding that every encounter results in an alteration of historical truth. Individuals look into the past to revisit loved ones or to bring to light new material that may have been overlooked. Her subjective decision to encounter the archive and rearticulate the

Edwards women's history in her poetry is what she defines as "mirror vision" (31). Mirror vision is looking at something that has already been seen by another, meaning it has already been interpreted. History then, is always seen through mirror vision. With each new encounter, a Xerox copy is made and becomes less like its original design. Although not entirely related, one could say that the self is constantly viewed in mirror vision because individuals project what they want to see onto themselves even if the architecture is not there to support the interpretation.

In addition to the presentation of the Edwards family archives and Howe's late husband's belongings, the fragmented, collage-style form comments on Howe's struggle to express her grief and the state of archives as collections of the past, gaping with missing information. First, "The Disappearance Approach" executes a fragmented interweaving of the speaker recounting the days before, the day of, and the days following her husband's death with exposition on the Edwards family, memories, metaphysical and linguistic rhetoric, literary allusions, and the painter Nicholas Poussin. Each stanza-like fragment is offset by a centered dash. More often than not, the accounts of Peter before and after death tend to be much shorter than the exposition on other topics. For example, on page nineteen, the speaker only gives five lines to the memory of taking the sleep apnea mask off her husband's face, but not two pages later she dedicates two and a half pages to the Edwards family archive. Interestingly enough, the sleep apnea, which is a "disorder characterized by pauses in breathing during sleep" is a perfect metaphor for the unreliability of archives as a complete account of the past (13). The breaks in continuous breathing represent the moments that fail to be preserved in archives. It also feels as if the pauses in breathing mirror the speaker's inability to articulate further on the loss of her husband.

Moreover, this abruption in form not only highlights the speaker's struggle to relay her personal loss, but it also shows that Howe's "poems [reveal] just how mediated language, history, and knowledge actually are" (Creasy). Much like how archivists are in control of what goes into a collection, Howe controls what the reader is allowed to see, both in her personal life and also in the historical information she provides to the reader. From the choice of the Edwards family down to the most unimportant word, Howe has mediated what the reader can see. Howe carefully constructs the layering of material; she does not want the poetry to unify the different threads, rather, she means to present "a chain of discordant, jarring testimonies" to demonstrate what history really looks like in an archive and in life (Crown, 484). The reader is allowed to witness the fallibility of memory and archive through Howe's fragmented form. The interruptive form of this section concludes with the speaker saying, "I often have the sense of intruding an infinite and finite local evocated and wonder how things are, in relation to how they appear" (34). In context, the line refers to Howe returning home after being away for a few days. The speaker is aware that nothing is what it seems to be. Even though she knows that the house was left in a certain way, she knows her memory is not totally reliable. Could this be the way she feels about archives that she revisits? What changes occur to an archive while she is away from them? It seems that upon visiting an archive, one intrudes on the past. Moreover, Howe use of the word "intruding" corresponds to the form and the content within the form. The form, which is wholly interruptive can also be seen as intruding upon the ability to form complete, coherent thoughts or statements. An intrusion prohibits clear sight of what is in front of the reader.

    Intrusion or interruption unfolds into the second section "Frolic Architecture" in a much more physical way. Howe copied, pasted, and taped text over one another. Even traces of the invisible scotch tape were left behind during the copying process of the project. Howe states in an interview with *The Paris Review* that with "Frolic Architecture" she "was constructing what [she] thought was a collaged text" that overlapped the Edwards family writings and her own journal entries. The result of this collage-style form is bits and pieces of writing popping off the page with other snippets being occluded from view. Words are cut off as Howe "trims the edges of the journal and overlaps lines to obscure them and prevent a clear reading" (Semonvitch). This occluded view functions several ways. First, it solidifies the argument that archives are unreliable sources of the past. As I demonstrated earlier, if a person relies on the written traces of the past, she is only getting the partial truth, and thus the present becomes skewed. The present is only allowed to witness the past after others have heavily mediated the relics curated within an archive. Moreover, the interruptive form functions like eavesdropping. Since the archival is a scattered account of history with certain voices being preserved, and other voices being lost to the void of time, those who encounter archived materials perform a sort of eavesdropping on history. When we engage with history, only certain voices are audible much like when we overhear a conversation. However, what I find most interesting about this fragmented form is that Howe points out that "everything appears in a deliberately constructed manner as if the setting of our story was always architectural" (15). She had made this statement upon thinking how everything in her life with Peter was constructed based on their individual pasts. The words "constructed" and "architectural" build upon the idea of the past controlling the present. Thus, she is arguing that the identity of the present self is wholly mediated by what came before it. Archives, dead spouses and half-true history mediates and continually revises ideas of the present. The process of this development becomes a tangible reality in the incoherent form of "Frolic Architecture." Evidence of Howe obstructing the reader's view is evident because traces of the tape are left behind on the paper. Howe could have figured out another way to compile the project, but I think she wanted shadows to be left behind because it physically demonstrates the mediation of what readers engage with not only in books, but also in the archives of loved ones and history. We are only allowed to see what others want us to see.

Susan Howe's collection *That This* is an incredibly complicated collection that leaves readers questioning their own identities and the past. Libraries and other institutions in control of archives are supposed to give an unclouded view of history, but Howe shatters that sense of comfort. And she does not do it solely to point blame at those in charge of archives; rather, she does it to point out the possibility that everybody is responsible for occluding history's truths. The remnants left behind by ancestors and loved ones provide resources for the living to use to engage with the past to form an understanding of existence and of identity. Howe weaves the loss of her husband with the misrepresented facts of the Edwards family to show that it is impossible to truly account for history, because those in charge of curating an archive are susceptible to their own desires without even knowing it. Moreover, family relics are personal and the voices of the past become tangible traces when one chooses to engage and converse with the belongings. While Howe's content and form highlight the inability to ever know oneself, to knowthe past, or to fully grasp the idea of existence, her collection succeeds in demonstrating that the personal and emotional connection with the past is more important than knowing the whole truth. After all, do we ever really know each other? Do we ever really know ourselves? Or have we already been decided upon by the architectural construction of the past?

Seamus Heaney's "Bog Queen": Ireland's Resistance to Historical Prejudice

> who veiled me again
> and packed coomb softly
> ……………………………
> ……………………………
>
> Till a peer's wife bribed him.
> The plait of my hair
> a slimy birth-cord
> of bog, had been cut
>
> And I rose from the dark,

The violent exploitation of Ireland by England during The Troubles is the main premise within Seamus Heaney's poem "Bog Queen." More importantly, the poem wrestles with the theme of resistance to historical prejudice. Heaney's poem elicits visceral images that depict the resurrection of an ornately dressed female bog body (the jewels to insinuate that she was of great wealth). Prior to the passage indicated above, the poem elaborately describes the physical body of the bog woman (from the voice of the bog queen) being uncovered by the turfcutter who pays his respects to the woman after this abrupt discovery. However, through a bribe he betrays the bog queen, leaving her to rise and seek vengeance on those who have betrayed her in the past. The violent tone married with the strong language signify that the bog queen stands for Ireland. Furthermore, the prior mistreatment by England (and betrayal by some Irishmen) will serve as the beginning of the rise of the Irish to regain equality. Through tone, and symbolic language, Seamus Heaney's poem "Bog Queen" uses the exploitation of Ireland to argue that historical prejudice serves as the stepping-stone for the resistance of a culture against external forces.

    While the tone in the first three-quarters of "Bog Queen" is empathetic, there is an abrupt shift to a violent tone between stanzas twelve and thirteen. For example, the turfcutter "packed coomb softly," this illustrates that the man attempts

to protect her by placing her back in the bog
after being stripped of her belongings
(Heaney, l. 46). He gently reburies her.
Since the bog woman stands for Ireland, a
country that was culturally assaulted by
England this line empathizes with the
turbulent treatment of the bog woman by
trying to repair the damage through
replacing her in her original state. However,
the tone shifts with "Till a peer's wife bribed
him," and the tone becomes that of betrayal
as the bog woman details her hair being
"cut" and taken from her without permission
(49 and 52). This prejudice against the bog
woman after the turfcutter had respected her
sparks a violent vengeance in the bog
woman/Ireland as she "rose from the dark"
in fervor to resist this act of violence against
her (53). This act of exploitation against the
bog woman forces her up to revolt against
the men and women who seek to strip her of
her hair, which very much symbolizes her
connection to her homeland, as it was the
anchor keeping her in the land. Arguably,
the empathetic tone shifts to a violent one as
the bog woman was nearly at rest once again
when somebody else chose to cut her from

the characteristics that identify her as the bog queen.

The symbolic language within "Bog Queen" aids the transition from the empathetic to violent tone, as well as bears striking connotations that lend to the theme of resistance against historical prejudice. The diction in "Bog Queen" is two-fold: the connotation of the nouns and the selection of verbs to describe the action. First, the nouns are "coomb" (46), "peer's wife" (49), "plait" (50), and "birth-cord" (51). The word "coomb" connotes the chalk downs of Ireland, which is a physical characteristic of the land. To pack the bog woman in a physical structure of Ireland suggests that she is a part of the land and removing her from it would sever her from her past. Thus, the diction lends to the empathetic tone and it argues that the turfcutter is aware that this woman has a nation and a history that exists regardless of the uncovering of her body. Heaney situates that body in her physical history in order to give rise to resistance as she is severed from her homeland in the violent cutting of her hair. Moreover, the term "peer's wife" suggests that the turfcutter was sexually bribed to cut the "plait" from the bog woman. Since peer is equivalent to friend, it works well with the concept of manipulating relations to achieve a goal, as the English did with Ireland's people during the national conflicts. This manipulation raises the tone of betrayal as the reader witnesses the bog queen's "plait", an intertwining braid of hair being cut from her body and separating her from the past prejudices committed against her. Furthermore, the noun, "birth-cord" solidifies the natural connection between the woman and her motherland. Her hair serves as the umbilical cord between her and her land. This sparks the bog woman to rise from the bog and seek vengeance on those who have attempted to separate her from her land and her culture. Not only does the cutting of the braid signify historical prejudice against the woman/Ireland, but also it allows the woman/Ireland to stand up and resist any further exploitation of the land that is home.

    As the nouns provide insight to the theme by adding to the tone of the poem, the action verbs, "veiled" (45) and "bribed"

(49), create the violent change from the bog woman passively lying in the land to actively resisting those who have attempted to keep her oppressed. The term "veiled" is strong in that the bog woman was brought up from the bog, her valuables were taken, and then those who brought her to the surface put her back in the bog and "veiled" her from the world. Her eyes are covered, and she cannot fight for her own rising from the dark. The term "veiled" in this line sounds similar to the cliché "pull the wool over your eyes" in that external forces are hiding the truths of the exploitation from the bog queen. The word symbolizes those who are veiling the woman, as well as those who are choosing to put a veil over their own eyes in order to avoid seeing the destruction of their country and their people. The connotation of "veiled" segues into "bribed," another manipulative verb within stanzas twelve and thirteen. The verb "bribed" suggests that there is a value threshold for the turfcutter to betray his bog queen. In this line, a woman seduces him with a bribe (money or sex) in order to get a hold of the powerful braid that connects the bog woman to the boglands. To be bribed suggests a weakness within the framework of the people of the land in that they are not strong enough to support their own land; however, this demonstrates that Ireland's historical past (or any historical prejudice) impacts the country's ability to stand up to those that have taken advantage of the people. This bribe is the mechanism that enables the land to regain itself. By succumbing to the bribe, the turfcutter releases the "veiled" queen, which indirectly leads to her "[rise] from the dark" (51). These final lines are a warning of resistance should any person attempt to veil the bog queen or her people in the future.

    The theme of historical prejudice on a people or a land and the rise of a resistance are strong throughout the "Bog Queen" as Heaney examines the impacts of the conflicts in Ireland regarding the position of Northern Ireland. In "Bog Queen," the bog woman serves as the physical and cultural land that has been exploited by England. Moreover, the violent tone and symbolic language suggest a political warning to those who have violated the bog queen's land in the past.

The Dream Songs: Double-Talk and Sexual Repression in Society during the 1950s and 1960s

The erotic, sexual repression developed throughout John Berryman's *The Dream Songs* not only exposes his erotic desires and megalomania, but it also highlights the societal atmosphere of the 1950s and 1960s. This era marks the beginning of extreme conformity and laws against outsiders within society. In response to the Cold War, the start of the Civil Rights Movement, and the counterculture, repression of sexuality among other pieces of individuality became a central focus. *The Dream Songs* perplex notions of love and desire through the development of double-talk between the sexually repressed protagonist Henry and the interjection of the interlocutor, Mr. Bones. The double-talk works to demonstrate the relationship between the sexually repressed population of American society and the governing body of society setting norms for sexuality. As the tensions grew tight with the onset of the Cold War, the Civil Rights Movement, and the tightening of American culture into a group of "appropriate" norms, those with alternative sexualities (homosexual, biracial preferences, etc.) became sexually repressed. Henry is a sexually charged character, repressed by society, who gropes at every chance to fulfill his erotic desires. Sexually, he is never fulfilled because society prevents him from acting on his urges. Mr. Bones' interlocutions remind Henry that society rejects him, and he would find himself persecuted if he were to act on his sexual desires. "Dream Song 3: A Stimulant for an Old Beast," "Dream Song 4," "Dream Song 10," and "Dream Song 69" highlight the persistent juxtaposition of Henry's fantasy world with reality that demonstrates his sexual urges and ultimate sexual repression. The poems are erotic yet focus on the repression of individual sexuality through tones of comedy and tragedy. Moreover, the diction and voice along with mechanics and odd syntactical units continue to expose Henry's sexual repression. Additionally, Berryman uses double-talk between Henry and Mr. Bones to expose the societal oppressors of sexuality. The techniques repress Henry, ultimately reflecting the sexual repression of the era. In "Dream Song 3," "Dream Song 4," "Dream Song 10," and "Dream Song 69;" John Berryman's use of persona, dismantled syntax, language, and mechanics illustrate Henry's erotic delusions and sexual repression that represent the sexual repression of Americans between the 1950s and 1960s.

  Before one can unravel the sexual repression represented in the persona, enjambment, and syntax of *The Dream Songs*, the reader must understand the double-talk within the poems. Every poem has at least two speakers, most often Henry and Mr. Bones. Identifying who is speaking comes down to dialect and a sense of syntax. For example, Henry often speaks with correct grammar, such as "I hungered back" in "Dream Song 4," or strange syntactical units. Moreover, Henry usually speaks in the first person. On the other hand, Mr. Bones speaks in a dialect similar to that of blackface that stems from the minstrel shows that were popular up until the mid-twentieth century. The dialect is quickly identified in most poems, similar to "This' hard work, / boss, wait'" in which there is the use of apostrophe to address Henry (Song 10). His grammar is muddled, for example, there are errors in the subject-verb agreement, such as "The enemy are sick," and he hardly ever enters a poem in first person (Song 10). The syntax of Mr. Bones, as well as his choice of words is filled with odd layers of meaning, which will be fleshed out further on in this paper. The double-speak serves many functions for the underlying meanings of each poem. Berryman creates the two personas to create a dialogue between the sexually repressed and the oppressive force. According to Adam Beardsworth's article "The Poetics of Double-talk: John Berryman's Dream Songs as Cold War Testimonials," to double-speak functions as a "metacommentary on 1950s and 1960s" cultural atmosphere and societal tensions (33). Hence, Henry wholly represents the repressed American sexualities, while Mr. Bones is the society that will not allow for men and women to express their individual love and desire. The double-speak cannot be discussed alone, as it intertwines with the other characteristics of Berryman's poetry.

    The dismantled syntax reveals Henry's sexual fantasies and the sexual repression that he endures in a society that does not accept his sexuality, which stands for the overall repression of American sexuality. The double-talk functions as a code in combination with the fragmented syntactical units lend to the contextual sexual repression of Henry and his urgent desires. For example, in "Dream Song 4," Henry is in turmoil over a desired woman he cannot have, so Mr. Bones interjects, "is stuffed, / de world, wif feeding girls" to give Henry reprieve from his deflated fantasy of devouring this woman across the table. But the interlocution of Mr. Bones also puts Henry back into the confinements of society. The double-speak and Henry's perceived idea of the statement numbs the unaccepted sexuality with "a sense of domestic agency" that subjects the offender (Henry) to possible persecution (Beardsworth, 34). The statement reminds him that his sexuality is neither appropriate, nor is it socially acceptable for the setting. Moreover, the line is out of order and should read as "the world is stuffed with feeding girls," but the disorder allows the line to be interpreted in a number of ways. Henry can hear it as there being many women to stuff, or he can hear that the world is full of women waiting to feast with Henry. In the last stanza of "Dream Song 4," Henry begins to fantasize again, asking, "What wonders is / she sitting on, over there?" The syntax forces the statement to question whether or not Henry is referencing the chair or referencing her genitalia. The broken unit of language allows Henry to sink further into his sexual fantasies, but Mr. Bones enters at the last minute with "There is" to remind Henry that there are laws against his sexual desires (Song 4). Not only does Mr. Bones serve as Henry's perceived protector against legal trouble, but he functions as the oppressor who "bullies [Henry] into a state of conformity that effectively castrates" him into the appropriate behavior allowed in society (Beardsworth, 36). The relationship is similar to that of Americans in the

1950s/1960s who were forced to hide their sexual orientation or relationships that were deemed inappropriate in the tense American culture of the period. Additionally, in "Dream Song 10," there is an odd syntactical interlocution from Mr. Bones that represents the sexually repressed. In response to the black man being hung for having a "tryst" with a white woman, Mr. Bones states, "The enemy are sick, / and so is us of" (Song 10). The double-speak here codes the American sentiment of confined sexuality through the "gnarled syntax and ruptured grammaticisms," without directly stating it to the enemy (Beardsworth, 32). The line refers to lynching that occurred during this era and quietly suggests a revolt against the oppressors that refuse to allow other forms of love and desire to occur between individuals of America.

    Moreover, throughout "Dream Song 3," "Dream Song 4," and "Dream Song 69" the radical enjambment provokes the sexual repression, while intensifying the crude oppression of sexuality. For example, in "Dream Song 69," Berryman enhances the repression by not allowing Henry to love the woman; he can only have sexual thoughts about the woman. His desires are heightened until the reader discovers that his sexual desires are about an "unconscious / woman" (Song 69). Not only does Berryman fracture his "metrical pattern" through this radical enjambment, but he also forces Henry into a dark place of sexual repression to the point that he fantasizes over a nonresponsive person (Beardsworth, 37). Henry is pushed to a point that could only be caused by severe sexual repression, much like that experienced during the height of the 1950s due to the rising tensions of the Cold War. The radical enjambment is further witnessed in "Dream Song 3: A Stimulant for an Old Beast," in which another woman and the poem thwart Henry's sexuality. Henry is erotically stimulated by the "lovely 23," yet he is put "out in the cold, / unkissed" in the following lines. Henry is numbed by the cold and the enjambment of "unkissed" on the next line serves as rejection. The poem makes a departure from here and moves into another subject which demonstrates "his loss of love and ... renders him flaccid," so Henry cannot return to his sexual desires for the young woman (Beardsworth, 35). If the rejection was not enough to confine Henry's sexuality, Berryman's interlocutor says, "As I said,—" to completely isolate Henry from society. Henry is "further destabilized by the incursions of his interlocutors" and must remain alone with his sexuality that is societally unacceptable (Beardsworth, 35). The interlocutor successfully thwarts Henry's sexuality, but the combination of the comma and em dash dismantle Henry from attempting to revolt against his oppressor, as he is not allowed to finish his own confession.

      While "Dream Song 3" and "Dream Song 69" push Henry and American sexuality deeper into repression, the enjambment in "Dream Song 4" also intensifies Henry's sexual repression through radical delusions. His delusions spark from the continuous sexual repression. In "Dream Song 4," a woman is eating in a restaurant and Henry fantasizes over her, momentarily believing that she desires him in return. Henry states, "She glanced at me / twice." The radical enjambment followed by the choice to put "twice" on its own line demonstrates the intensity of this moment for Henry, as well as his inability to perceive social cues. His absurd sexual obsession over a woman who looked at him highlights the damage caused to persons under severe psychological stress and "repressive state policies" (Beardsworth, 32). If Henry were allowed to express his sexuality, he may not interpret this scene with such vigor. However, his fantasy does not last long; he plummets into erotic despair as his urge to spring "on her" is destroyed by heavy enjambment into a new stanza, leaving Henry's only option to be "falling at her little feet and crying" (Song 4). The new stanza forces Henry to abandon his sexual urges and become aware of the lines that confine him into a society that refuses his individual sexuality, much like American citizens who had to hide their own sexuality during the 1950s and 1960s. Beardsworth notes that Americans suffering from sexual repression similar to Henry are "tormented by persecution" as they are unable to fulfill personal needs in public settings (34). Thus, the sexually repressed code their desires through heightened fantasies, yet cannot express them without being rejected by society.

      The mechanics and syntax of the poems allow the double-talk to demonstrate the sexual struggles of Henry, yet the persona/voice within Berryman's poetry with respect to tone and word choice expose Henry's thwarted sexuality and persistent persecution by the oppressive interlocutions. For example, in "Dream Song 10," the speaker says, "A vote would come / that would be no vote," which proves that regardless of what the collective body of America desires, oppressive forces will make the ultimate decision. Henry, or this man who is being lynched in "Dream Song 10," does not get a free pass for acting on his sexuality—a sexuality that is not accepted by those who make the rules. In this case, it is because a black man who chose to have a sexual relationship with a white woman, as discerned by "to rising trysts." During the 1950s, black men were lynched for having relationships with white women. The "ambiguous forces of persecution" act to oppress sexual relationships or desires that do not coincide with the current social and political atmosphere of the era (Beardsworth, 35). Individuals were forced to hide their relationships or not have them at all, which leads to the sexual fantasies and repressive behavior seen in Henry's persona.

This repressive nature is understood through the dark, comedic, yet depressing voice throughout the poems that expose Henry's sexual rejection. In "Dream Song 3," after Henry ends up "unkissed" by the "lovely 23" the interlocutor remarks, "(— My psychiatrist can lick your psychiatrist) Women get under / things." The parenthetical interlocution yields a comical tone to ease the sexual rejection of being out in the cold. The parenthesis further isolate Henry, which shows the forced repression of "individual autonomy" and one's sexual behavior (Beardsworth, 35). The sexually driven words demonstrate Henry's struggle to cope with the reality of his sexual repression in the event of rejection by women (and society) that do not accept his alternative desires. Henry chooses to put women under things because he cannot handle the constant sexual rejection. The tone falls into despair because it is empty of all love and desire that embodies Henry. This despairing tone continues in "Dream Song 69," in which the speaker (possibly Mr. Bones) reveals that Henry does not love a woman, "but the thought he puts / into that young woman" is so large that it would launch an international campaign. The interlocution used to introduce Henry's state of mind works to separate Henry from society, while also highlighting his sexual repression. The word choice of "puts into" is sexualized to show that even Henry's thoughts about women are repressed. His impulses toward sexual freedom are "beyond cultural concern" at this point because he has been rendered immobile in his ability to love in a way that is socially acceptable (Beardsworth 33). He cannot put into words the exact sexual desire that he feels, nor can he love her. Society has beaten Henry in the fight between rules and autonomy; the interlocution functions as the oppressor and the reminder of being sexually thwarted.

    Furthermore, the language in "Dream Song 4" continues the sexually charged tension and adds more evidence that the tone and word choices are exposing the double-talk that represents Henry's sexual repression and the societal pressure against him to conform to the sexual norms. For example, the woman is "filling her compact & delicious body" while eating chicken. Henry fantasizes over the woman in a way that her eating represents him feasting on the women (or perhaps sexuality in general) that he cannot attain. He deludes into his fantasy world where everybody is sexually liberated, until the interlocution by Mr. Bones reminds him that there are plenty of other women in the world that he could have. His desire to feast is thwarted again, and "he is being inflicted with both physical and psychological violence" by Mr. Bones, and by extension, society (Beardsworth, 35). The social climate physically prevents him from being sexually involved with women due to cultural regulations, while psychologically he prevents himself due to the persistent attacks on his sexual desires by Mr. Bones. In this case, Mr. Bones functions as Henry's oppressor and protector from the law, as he reminds Henry that there is "a law against

[him]" (Song 4). Henry is not free to express his sexuality and when he does think about his own desires, he is reminded that it is not acceptable. The coercions into conformity are so powerful that he cannot see that it is the very sexual repression by his oppressor that has forced him to view his needs as something that must be chained up to protect others (Beardsworth, 35). Not only does Henry understand that society is thwarting his sexuality, but he has been pushed down so many times that he actually believes that his sexuality is wrong.

The Dream Songs work to create a double-talk that demonstrates the impact of sexual repression in a tense cultural atmosphere. The 1950s and 1960s were marked with tightened social laws (both directly and indirectly) that outlawed alternative sexualities or thwarted sexual desires that did not align with the present political and cultural ideologies. The use of interlocution to remind Henry of his unaccepted sexuality and desires illustrate the impact of sexual repression on all Americans during the 1950s and 1960s. Unfortunately, the extreme sexual repression creates people who cannot function properly within society. Henry's sexual delusions and deep sexual repression represent the painful experiences of all Americans who faced sexual repression by society. Berryman uses comedic and depressing tones to perplex the actions and words of the poems. Each poem exacerbates the sexual suffering that Henry faces, while using double-talk to juxtapose the sexually repressed with the oppressor. He has been rejected so many times that he has becomes sexually deluded in public situations and begins to believe what his oppressor is saying about his sexuality. He ceases to love women, in turn using them as sexual fantasies or degrading them when he feels denied. Moreover, the brash use of punctuation and enjambment allow the delusions and thwarted sexuality to surface between the content and form of "Dream Song 3," "Dream Song 4," "Dream Song 10," and "Dream Song 69." The remainder of *The Dream Songs* work towards the same goals in an effort to expose the interlocutor of Henry's repressed sexuality. The interlocution of Mr. Bones serves to balance the deluded desires and depressing rejection with awareness of one another in reality. He seeks to ease Henry's pain and keep him stationed in reality. Henry will not escape the sexual repression of a society that chooses to box him in unless he actively seeks to destroy the interlocutor—but this cannot happen since he lives in a society that refuses to accept his sexual being.

Fragmented Voices of a Whole

<u>The Dream Songs</u> by John Berryman highlights the search for identity of self and of America. Berryman sets up the songs to be the dreams of Henry, a black man and often in the format of a Minstrel Show performance. There are varying voices that switch between white and black dialects. These voices are coming from inside Henry's mind who is searching for his own unified identity within a society that is fragmented and unaccepting of his personhood. Berryman uses these minstrelsy personas to highlight the racial ideology created by whiteness, in a hope to dismantle the burdens placed on African Americans. The poetic voice is incredibly important in *The Dream Songs* because it acts as a deconstruction of "blackness" and "whiteness" to demonstrate that identity does not (or should not) include the social construct of race. Berryman disguises himself underneath the multiplicity of voices that Henry has created as a result of a departure that has created division within his

self, as well as the overall division of the multi-culture, multi-dialect conglomerate that is America. The theme of a fractured self/society that is desperately seeking solidarity resonates throughout the Dream Songs. Moreover, it seems that Henry is a symbol for America, which Berryman demonstrates through the voice pronouns, "I," "we," "us," and "one," while casting the pronouns "they" and "them" as the forces acting against an America that is unified without racial parameters. John Berryman's Henry in *The Dream Songs* is a voice that is fragmented into a multitude of voices searching for a unified identity, which is performed on stage as a Minstrel Show. Henry symbolizes the disunited American culture, as well as the poetic voice seeking to deconstruct "whiteness" in order to tear down racial oppression.

    Berryman demonstrates that Henry has departed from a former, less-damaged self in exchange for a multitude of voices or "selves" as he seeks to find an identity. This identity is mangled by the oppression of whites during the 1950–1960s. "Dream Song 1" sets up the departure that Henry experiences throughout his dreams as he lives the lives of many sorts of selves. For example, it is said that Henry is "trying to put things over" in regards to something that has happened on "the day" that "Huffy Henry hid" (Song 1, ll. 1–3). Henry endured a major conflict that caused suffering, forcing him to hide it deep within himself. It is clear that Henry departed from his original self (perhaps his more innocent self), since Berryman writes that the world "once did seem on Henry's side" and that "once in a sycamore tree I was glad," but "then came a departure" which Henry could never go back beyond again (Song 1, ll. 8, 9, 15). Henry's dislocation is a result of the occasion generative of speech that Grossman discusses in "Summa Lyrica," which discusses the occasional generative of speech as a dislocation or "disease" of the subject-object relationship. The impact of "the day" in "Song 1" causes Henry to divorce from the self, thereby forming a fragmented version of who he used to be. This fragmentation of self is Berryman's attempt at "bringing speech out of the silence" and proving to the academy that racial ideology is unnecessary.

The voices that develop from the suffering/disease in "Song 1" are present throughout *The Dream Songs*, but they are fully confirmed in "Song 2" (and in many other songs, too), which addresses Henry's ability to acknowledge the separate voices and divisions within his mind while trying to stay unified. It is important to note, that the term "division of self" in response to the voices that are created within Henry's mind are the product of the abandonment of the autonomy of the will (Grossman's "Immortality I," 1.2). Berryman/Henry has abandoned the autonomy of the will because he is dreaming, which is similar to stating that one is dead since a complete lack of present awareness is occurring while dreaming. Thus, the voices come out of the divorce of the self from the origin. In "Song 2," three voices become present: Henry, the African-American man; Mr. Bones, the man in blackface; and the friend, Sir Galahad. All three represent Henry, whether it is Henry speaking, Mr. Bones speaking of Henry, or the friend making a comment about the scene. Berryman gives cues to the poetic persona being aware of the divisions in "Song 2" when he says, "Henry are / baffled" rather than using the singular version of the verb "to be" (Song 2, ll. 4–5). Here, the reader witnesses Henry as a multiplicity of voices/selves that is seeking to find an identity under the mind of one person. Furthermore, Henry acknowledges the divisions within his mind in "Song 28" stating, "where I am / we don't know." He is both singular and plural in nature. Henry harbors the voices of a fragmented identity.

There is evidence that Henry's fragmentation could have occurred from the dislocation of himself through Lacan's Mirror Stage, as well. The Mirror Stage occurs when one views oneself in the mirror and views the self as whole. However, one can no longer be whole because they have fragmented themselves into what they actually possess and what they see in the mirror. Moreover, it is the formation of the ego, which Lacan claims to be a misunderstanding the self. It is a process of identification. In *The Dream Songs*, the reader witnesses Henry viewing himself in the mirror several times. For example, in "Song 5," the speaker states, "Henry sats in de bar & was odd, / off in the glass from the glass" and in "Song 8" the speaker states, "They installed mirrors till he flowed." Moreover, in "Song 19" the speaker states, "Gentle friendly Henry Pussy-cat / smiled into his mirror." On all accounts, Henry is seeing himself as whole, but he knows that there are multiplicities within; thereby he is aware that he is fragmented, too. This fragmentation is not caused by the development of his identity; rather it is caused by the parameters of racial oppression forcing the construct of "black" onto his identity. This is where he becomes a fragmented self in search of an identity. *The Dream Songs* illustrates a man that suffers and endures similarly to his "white" counterparts, yet he must endure more because in the mirror he is "black."

 Henry's dive into a multitude of voices and his fractured self, while trying to preserve solidarity, demonstrates Henry's attempt to locate his identity in the face of internal and external struggles. During *The Dream Songs* Henry fights with the internal desire to find an identity and the external force of society on him as a "black" male in a "white" society. For example, in "Song 13," it is decided that Henry is "a human being" and "a human American man," while in "Song 16" Henry's skin is referred to as a "pelt" and to have a "long and glowing tail." This discrepancy illustrates that Henry's identity is somewhere in between a man with agency and an animal with human-like qualities. These are the external forces pushing against Henry's ability to successfully form a fully-functioning identity that is valued as highly as a person to be considered a full American person (white men). Furthermore, there are two instances within "Song 4" and "Song 10" which prove that Henry is struggling internally and externally. In "Song 4," Henry wants to spring on a woman, however he states, "There ought to be a law against Henry. /—Mr. Bones: there is." Henry determines that there is an internal morality stopping him from sexually assaulting the woman as well as an external law against it. Likewise, in "Song 10," Henry is being lynched because he was carrying on an interracial relationship with a white woman: "to rising trysts, / like this one, drove he out." Society is dictating to Henry that due to his skin color, he is not allowed to date a "white" woman. There is an instance in *The Dream Songs*, in which Henry celebrates himself: "Song 22." He says, "I am Henry Pussycat! Let my whiskers fly." This line is similar to that of Whitman's "I celebrate myself" in "Song of Myself." It is celebratory, but in rhetoric, which is due to the stage that Berryman places the dreams of Henry.

The voices that are heard throughout *The Dream Songs*, regardless of the internal/external struggles are a symbol of the citizens of American society during Berryman's time. In "Song 8," the speaker says, "They took away his teeth" and "they blew out his loves," which refers to white men oppressing black people. Berryman is demonstrating the oppressive force that racial ideology has on African-American people during the 1950–1960s. On the other hand, in "Song 22," Henry states that he is a multitude of different people: "I am the little man who smokes & smokes / I am so wise I

had my mouth sewn shut / I am the enemy
of the mind / I am a governmental official &
a goddamned fool / I am the blackt-out
man." None of these characters has
something terribly in common with another,
except for the fact that they are nobody
important. Furthermore, they are all
representative of an America that has
nothing uniting its citizens and is wholly
fractured. "Song 22" represents the
antithesis of Whitman's "Song of Myself."
Berryman pens a morose and divided nation
that is struggling to find its identity, much
like that of Henry's self-quest. On the other
hand, Whitman is celebrating himself and
American society. Whitman draws a
respectable and loving relationship between
the "I" of the individual and the "I" of
America. Additionally, Berryman uses
Henry as a symbol for America in "Song
13," stating, "God bless Henry" and that "he
lived like a rat" to illustrate that Henry is
America. It shows that he is living like them
already, so why isn't he given the same
treatment? The rats are the white people. He
provides a paradox: Henry deserves the
same treatment as white people, and that all

men and women like Henry form the American society. That they deserve the same recognition as the white men who are oppressing them. Berryman's rhetoric is used to highlight Henry's actual identity as "a human American man" and his identity as white America's racial ideology.

Berryman puts the voices of Henry into a minstrelsy performance to show the varying dialects created by white men and projected on black people, and to show how performing what black people are supposed to be like is the very racial oppression that needs to be eliminated. He is deconstructing whiteness and blackness by putting the confessions of a white man underneath a character that is in blackface and is black. *The Dream Songs* are set in the time when the minstrel show was developing and becoming popular in the United States. The citizens that moved from the rural regions into the urban regions were forced to create a new culture that was multi-cultural. They needed to create a culture that made them feel like family. According to The Emergence of a "Common Man's Culture," the common people came together in theaters to sing, dance, and tell stories of how they visualized life (9). Since Henry's dreams are performed as a minstrel show, Berryman maintains the varying dialects to preserve the realness of how a Minstrel Show would work. Each of these voices; Henry, Mr. Bones, and the friend; are responsible for putting on a show that highlights the suffering of Henry in a comic fashion. The audience is meant to overhear the words that come out of the poetry because Mr. Bones wants the audience to feel the suffering that Henry is resolving. Concerning the minstrelsy dialects, Grossman states, "all poetic languages are versions of social language" and "when I speak of them as 'versions' I mean that we encounter them as disguises" (Summa Lyric, pt. 2). This resonates with the voices that fill Henry's head as being fragmented versions of his identity—of his current self. His interpretation of identity is disguised under the color of his skin. Moreover, this confusion of identity is precisely why Berryman chooses to do *The Dream Songs* as a white man in black face and from the perspective of a black man. Berryman can never know the suffering of racism on African Americans, but he can demonstrate that by confessing the life of a white man (Berryman himself) underneath blackface. Perhaps then society may be able to recognize that "whiteness" and "blackness" are cultural phenomena that hinder society. Berryman points out that blackness is created by whiteness. White men performing as black men created the dialects themselves. Berryman chooses to perform *The Dream Songs* in minstrelsy to show that the performance itself is racial oppression, as it wrongly illustrates the identities of African-American citizens.

The Dream Songs is enigmatic with myriad functions in the realm of racial oppression and American society. It demonstrates that the identity is fragmented and constantly seeking to assimilate itself with an interpretation of itself. Henry's life is performed on the minstrel stage to show that the racial dialects and the sufferings of his life are not in need of a racial signifier. Berryman created Henry to prove that whiteness and blackness do not exist; rather they are a cultural product of society attempting to police others who do not fit within one's idea of identity. Moreover, *The Dream Songs* are used to show that a person can maintain unity under circumstances of fracture, which includes individuals and society. Lastly, the minstrel show performance is used to deconstruct blackness by deconstructing whiteness.

Eliot's Thwarted Lovers: An Allusion to Tristan and Isolde

In T.S. Eliot's *The Wasteland*, he makes an allusion to the thwarted lovers in Wagner's operatic version of Tristan and Isolde to highlight the absence of love in the barren setting of the modern world. The allusion is made in "The Burial of the Dead," the narrator states,

> Frisch weht der Wind
> Der Heimat zu
> Mein Irisch Kind,
> Wo Weilest du?
> (Eliot, ll. 31–34)

The song translates to "Fresh blows the wind / To the homeland / My Irish child / Where do you wait?" which is overheard in the opera by Isolde who believes that her love for Tristan is unreciprocated, leading her to attempt to kill herself with poison (and Tristan too). Fortunately, Isolde's nurse swaps the poison for a love potion, allowing them to fall in love with each other. However, Tristan is mortally wounded, and he dies after a watch man tells him, "Oed und leer das Meer," which translates to "Desolate and empty is the sea," implying that Isolde was not coming to meet him (line 42). Afterwards, Isolde arrives to find Tristan dead and dies of a broken heart. The romantic allusion of thwarted lovers is one of many instances within *The Wasteland* in which Eliot demonstrates that the industrialized world consistently frustrates and hinders divine or emotional love. Furthermore, Eliot repurposes the story of Tristan and Isolde to emphasize the melancholic theme that resounds throughout the entire poem; Eliot feeds off the anticipation between the lovers to exemplify the setting's relationship to life's inability to survive in this wasteland. There is a constant anticipation within the poem for spring to be born, yet Eliot constantly thwarts it with the "Unreal city" that is "Under the brown fog of winter dawn," much like the love between Tristan and Isolde (60–61). The morose setting juxtaposed with the lovers is an argument against the implications of modernity and industrialization. More importantly, Eliot manipulates the deception of the watch man telling Tristan that his lover will not meet with him; the sea, which should be full of life, is desolate. In other words, there is no love that can survive under the pressure and deception of modernity within society. The loss of humanity will thwart love, which is why this allusion is fitting for the poem as the combination of lost love and lost nature successfully argue against modernity. Eliot believes that love cannot be born or survive in the ever-changing environment of the modern world, so long as society seeks to push against true, divine love (or spirituality, thought, and rebirth). Ultimately, Eliot succeeds in using the allusion of Tristan and Isolde to illustrate that modernity can interfere with the development of nature, love, and humanity.

Wordsworth and Whitman: Awakening of Selfhood in Silence

The awakening of the self is present in Walt Whitman's "Out of the Cradle Endlessly Rocking" and his predecessor William Wordsworth's "Nutting." Wordsworth envisions a self that is developed through an encounter with nature, while Whitman carves out a self by merging nature and others into the self (known as intersubjectivity). The narrator of each poem experiences coming-of-age in the setting of a silent nature setting. The silence starts the poem, harbors the self through the journey from dormant to alive, and ends with silence as the narrator moves beyond the former self. Wordsworth's "Nutting" is a fantastical poem of a young boy embarking on a journey in which he takes in all of the magnificent nature around him, but then breaks out and tramples through the forest in search of hazelnuts. Moreover, Walt Whitman's "Out of the Cradle Endlessly Rocking" is the story of a boy who witnesses a male bird that laments over the loss of his significant other; the boy is able to translate the birdsong, thus learning about the realities of adulthood (life and death). Both poets point out that a childhood experience that includes a change from pure to tainted and from silence to noise shapes the rest of a young person's life. Whitman's decision to birth the self out of silence through the intertwined boy and bird is an attempt to revise Wordsworth's development of the self that encounters nature. The poems' uses of figurative language, such as word choice and imagery, as well as sound devices to demonstrate the journey from the innocent-self to the knowing-self comes out of silence.

    Whitman and Wordsworth use technical sound devices such as enjambment and caesuras to enact patterns of silence that frame the birth of the self of each narrator. Each poem begins with silence, breaks from the silence as the self is born, and resumes silence after the narrator recognizes the loss of his former self. For example, "Nutting" opens with "_____ — It seems a day / (I speak of one from many singled out)" (Wordsworth, 1–2) to highlight that the long pause combined with an em dash represents an absolute silence that frames the start of this coming-of-age journey. Moreover, the enjambment of the parenthetical statement frames the experience in silence as the man remembers the birth of his selfhood. Similarly, Whitman's narrative begins with enjambment and a caesura to signify a similar silence as the boy writes, "Over the sterile sand and the fields beyond, where the child / _____leaving his bed wandr'd alone" (Whitman, 4–5). The "sterile sands" represent the silence and purity of virginal nature (and the boy) before "leaving his bed" to immerse himself into the experience of the birdsong and into the birth of the self. The marriage of the caesuras and enjambment sets up the silence required of the self to awaken. The caesura of line five quiets the moment with a large breath before the boy continues his journey. Unlike Wordsworth who begins the journey in absolute silence, Whitman chooses to pair the absolute silence of the "sterile sands" with the unvoiced hissing of the fields at night to illustrate that they boy will reach manhood through a mediation of the silence with the noise.

As each poem progresses, the narrator travels through nature in silence (and in admiration of what they see/hear), until the silence is broken and the self is born. Wordsworth's narrator states, "And on the vacant air. Then up I rose" (Wordsworth, 43) in which the caesura splits the silence from the sound and, ultimately, the past self from the present self. The boy awakens in his destruction of nature and realizes that he is no longer a boy, but a man and states,

> Their quiet being: and, unless I now
> Confound my present feelings with the past;
> ....
> ......
> ....
> ....
> I felt a sense of pain when I beheld
> The silent trees, and saw the intruding sky— (48–53).

The boy looks upon what he has done to the woods and realizes that he cannot return to his boyhood. This lesson teaches him of the irreversible change that occurs when one learns something that informs about life. The enjambment between "now" and "confound" silences the loudness of the boy's self as it encountered the natural world. Furthermore, it represents the separation between the innocent self and the knowing self as the boy struggles in the silence of the aftermath of the destruction. Wordsworth reframes the new self in silence through multiple caesuras and enjambments, as the setting gets quiet around him as he witnesses the loss of his former innocence. The dash enacts a pattern of silence and the "intruding sky" (53) silences his ability to return to his boyhood. Moreover, the caesura helps to quiet the scene with the absolute silence in the trees. On the other hand, Whitman chooses to awaken the self through the hard lesson of loss (death) and uses sound techniques to illustrate the silence between the birdsong and the boy waiting for the message that the bird sings. The silence frames the scene through the caesura of the question mark and use of commas. For example, the boy states, "Listen'd to keep, to sing, now translating the notes" (Whitman, 70) while waiting for the message of the bird's lover. But upon finding out that she never returned he asks, "Is it indeed toward your mate you sing? or is it really to me?" (146). The narrator follows up with "Now in a moment I know what I am for, I am awake" (147), which shows that the narrator recognizes that the song not only relates to life and death, but to the loss of his childhood and the birth of his present self. Whitman emulates the sound devices of Wordsworth's "Nutting" to frame the birth of the self within silence (in which there is a juxtaposition of innocence and knowledge), yet the main difference is that Whitman seems to think that the silence truly awakens the self in the cycle of nature.

    While sound devices enact patterns of silence, Wordsworth and Whitman use imagery and word choice to portray the silence and absence of silence that births the self as one encounters and merges with nature. Wordsworth positions the narrator to encounter nature while Whitman integrates nature into the narrator. Wordsworth's narrator heads "Tow'rd some far-distant woods" (8) and that "Forcing my way, I came to one dear nook/unvisited, where not a broken bough" (16-17) and finds the "virgin scene" (21) in silence. For a moment, he admires the quiet nature and the words "distant" and "unbroken" make the scene silent, but the word "Forcing" is a sign that this innocence cannot remain as he encounters the silence before the birth of his selfhood. Upon the birth of the self, the silence disappears as the boy "dragged to the earth both branch and bough with crash" (44). The loud imagery interrupts the silence as the boy tears down the woods, thereby coming-of-age out of silence. At the end of the "merciless ravage" (45) the narrator learns that he has lost his boyhood in his choice to break the silence and that this loss cannot be reversed. He advises a young girl of this experience stating, "Touch—for there is a spirit in the woods" (56), and silence overcomes him as he remembers his own loss of innocence in hopes that the young girl will not make the same mistake.

Wordsworth shows that the self is born out of silence and through an encounter with nature, however Whitman revises these ideas by integrating the experience of the bird with the boy's self. Furthermore,

Whitman constructs silence between the bird and the boy with imagery and word choice to show that the self is born by merging the bird's sorrow and the boy's ability to translate the bird's words. For example, Whitman states, "Out of the Ninth-month midnight" (Whitman, 3) to demonstrate that out of the darkest silence, the self is born. The word "Out" combined with the birth of a baby initiates the beginning of selfhood from silence. As the boy progresses in to the birdsong, Whitman uses imagery and word choice of listening and the unheard voice of nature to prove the birth of the self from silence. The narrator "blending [himself] with the shadows" (65) waits for the bird to teach him of the loss and he "listen'd long and long" (69) for the words to break the silence. Upon the boy hearing the bird singing in search of his mate, the unvoiced hiss of "The aria's meaning" hits "the ears, the soul," (139) and the boy's self in the broken silence of "A thousand warbling echoes [that] have started a life in me" (155). The shadows, whispers, and unvoiced sorrows of the bird awaken the boy's ability to understand the song and transform him into a knowing-self that must come to terms with loss. Whitman's decision to translate the song within the boy veers away from Wordsworth's narrator who only encounters nature, but never makes it a part of his new self. Out of the silence the boy learns through intersubjectivity that his "own songs awakened from the hour" (79) in the moment that he meshed the bird's experience with his own experiences.

    Silence frames the birth of the self and the narrator realizes that the progression of life does not permit one to return to their more innocent self. William Wordsworth and Walt Whitman use silence to frame the coming-of-age experience of two young boys. Wordsworth uses the silence of the untouched woods to set up a narrator on the edge of becoming a young adult. The imagery, word choice, and sound devices allow the boy to be born into adulthood through an encounter with nature. On the other hand, Whitman uses these literary devices to create a narrator that develops nature within him to awaken the self as he grapples with the knowledge of reality. As a revisionary of Wordsworth, Whitman desires to show that all creatures can benefit from each other's experiences. Moreover, both narrators are awakened in the presence of silence as it frames the innocence beforehand and the new identity created at the end of each poem. The silence serves as a medium between the quiet innocence of children and the loud coming-of-age these boys' experience as they realize that life cannot stay stagnant. The question that remains is, can the whirring of knowledge that takes away the former self ever be truly silenced, or will the moment of the unvoiced hiss always remain?

Shifting Values of Courtesy: "Sir Gawain and the Green Knight"

Arthurian romances are deeply situated in the chivalric code, courtly love, and knighthood. Of the most common concepts written in these pieces, the act of courtesy is most prevalent. While the act of courtesy as a code of conduct showcases the importance of behavior in medieval courts, the superficiality of its use in "Sir Gawain and the Green Knight" indicates that the concept needed to be reevaluated. In the poem, courtesy functions within two roles: to uphold the reputation of a lord's court and to be used as a code of conduct to govern one's behaviors based on his/her position within the court. Moreover, the Gawain-poet uses the word "courtesy" (and behaviors enveloped by the term) to highlight courtly expectations, and to demonstrate how the extremeness of knights attempting to be perfectly courteous can interfere with one's virtues and/or beliefs if courtesy takes precedence. Sir Gawain, King Arthur's most esteemed knight, fights with his obligation to the code of courtesy and his desire to maintain his virtues and positions as a man who is pressing against the superficial nature of courtesy as King Arthur uses it. This shift from wholly accepted chivalric code to an undermining of its genuineness insinuates that the Gawain-poet was not simply presenting another King Arthur knight legend. The Gawain-poet uses verbal irony, figurative language, and character actions to expose the superficial mask of courtesy on the people in King Arthur's court in "Sir Gawain and the Green Knight," and, ultimately, rejects the current code of courtesy in favor of genuine behaviors.

  Courtesy functions as a code used to uphold the reputation of King Arthur's court and acts as a code of expectations for those within the court to adhere to in their lives. The first role is witnessed in the relationship between Arthur and the Green Knight, as well as through the interactions between Sir Gawain and Bertilak. For example, the Green Knight enters Arthur's court and demands to see the court's esteemed courtesy claiming that "your court and your company are counted the best" (l. 259). He continues, stating, "courtesy here is carried to its height" thereby provoking Arthur to prove his court's reputation by "graciously grant[ing] the game" (ll. 263 and 273). The Green Knight assumes that Arthur will oblige in the beheading game in order to uphold the reputation of his court being the most adherent to the chivalric code. Reputation is clearly measured by the amount of courtesy given to people with the court, as the use of the words "counted" and "carried" indicate that a court's reputation raises with the increase in courtesy toward others. Arthur must grant the game to prove his court's strict adherence to a code that masks the true desires of the men at the hall.

    The second instance in which courtesy is used to validate a court's reputation is during the meeting between Sir Gawain and Bertilak at Haut Desert. Gawain "courteously confessed that he comes from the court / And owns him of the brotherhood of… Arthur" (ll. 904–5). At the mention of Arthur, the people at Bertilak's court become wide-eyed and look on to see this gracious knight fulfill the expectations that they have created concerning Arthur's knights. According to Alan Markman in his article "The Meaning of "Sir Gawain and the Green Knight," the boasted reputation of Gawain "reflected the ideal of chevalerie which feudal age tried to maintain" (Markman, 576). Thus, Gawain's reputation and his behavior while at Bertilak's court becomes a direct display of the values of King Arthur's court. As a knight, Gawain must choose to be courteous and uphold his lord's expectations even if they do not come naturally to him or do not fit into his virtues/morals.

    Moreover, courtesy in Arthurian romance serves to govern the actions and behaviors of persons within the royal court. This role of courtesy is exemplified in the relationship between Gawain and Bertilak's wife. For example, in Fitt 3, Bertilak's wife attempts to seduce Gawain while her husband is out hunting, claiming that he should oblige her as it is a part of his courtesy. She remarks to Gawain, "And cannot act in company as courtesy bids," arguing that he must give in to her as it his duty to take part in courtly love and not to refuse her advances (l. 1483). Gawain finds himself in a predicament with courtesy, as he is to oblige to wife, yet honor Bertilak. It is an "extreme test of Gawain's loyalty," for which he determines that loyalty to the lord is the right decision (Markman, 584). In either case, Gawain must adhere to courtly codes that dictate his behavior or attempt to thrust him into a choice that goes against his desires. Markman portrays Gawain as the "perfection of knighthood," due to his keen adherence to courtesy throughout the poem. However, Gawain is merely a symbol that the poet uses to highlight the unreachable code of courtesy and the need to push away from it within society (578). The roles are inherent throughout the poem, but it is through literary techniques that the strict code of courtesy is outlined as superficial and ultimately rejected.

 Both aforementioned roles of courtesy are highlighted throughout the poem and slowly, the voice of the Gawain-poet illustrates a rejection of the prescribed courtesy as it can impede on one's virtues and decisions. Most commonly, the rejection is best seen through irony, figurative language, and character actions. The first example of rejection is the interaction between Arthur and the Green Knight. The Green Knight enters, and Arthur reacts arrogantly to his disturbance. The Green Knight says, "but as the praise of you, is puffed up so high" that he has come to see it for himself. (l. 258). The phrase "puffed up" means to be raised high in a pompous fashion and indicates that the Green Knight is stating it ironically. Perhaps, he knows that Arthur is quick to fight and use his knights in any game to prove his worth. Moreover, the Green Knight promises, "I pass here in peace, and part as friends," and he shows that he has no intention to bring harm (l. 266). Arthur responds brashly saying, "Sir Courteous Knight…You shall not fail to fight," even though the man stated that he was at the court in peace (ll. 277–78). While it seems that Arthur is acting to preserve his courtesy, the juxtaposition of contradictory words like "puffed up," "peace," and "Courteous" are used to point out that Arthur is more concerned with his pride. He is protecting "his sense of duty, or decorum," however it is selfish, unlike the nature of Sir Gawain who does it because if his dedication to his knightly virtues (Markman, 577). The code of courtesy superficially masks his warrior-like nature, and the poet is attempting to reject it through the verbal irony.

While verbal irony outwardly stresses the superficiality of courtesy in Arthur's court, the figurative language throughout the poem honors the virtue of courtesy but rejects its utopic standards in exchange for Sir Gawain's genuine actions. Sir Gawain and his fellow knights are expected to uphold the five virtues, yet the intersections between knighthood, courtly love, and one's own virtues complicate a knight's ability to fully follow the code of courtesy. For example, in the beginning of the poem, Gawain adamantly takes the place of Arthur in the beheading game, arguing "the loss of my life would be least of anything," as it is of the code of courtesy (and knighthood) to protect the reputation of his lord's court (l. 355). Here, the poet reveals the absurdity of courtesy, as Gawain would willingly give his life for his lord, a man who is arrogantly protecting his pride and not his people.

Markman suggests that "his willingness to accept the monstrous challenge" is inherent in Gawain's virtuous nature (577). Furthermore, it proves "what a splendid man Gawain is," yet it does not prevent Gawain from acting on his behalf (575). The actions are solely based on the artificial code of courtesy that a knight must protect his lord. Markman argues that the poet was highlighting a perfect knight, but this perfection comes alongside pride and unattainability which points in a different direction. Later in the poem, Gawain is noted as the "father of fine manners" at Bertilak's castle, which plays on the alliteration of those words (l. 919). If looked at from a religious standpoint, one could argue that the Gawain-poet was setting up the fall of Gawain through these words. By putting Gawain at the apex of knightly behavior, the poem opens up for the ability to reject superficial courtesy in exchange for humble humanity. The language suggests that Sir Gawain's perfection is the flaw; courtesy is subverting his true virtues, and Arthur affirms that courtesy is a mask through his abrasive words and actions.

The Gawain-poet further exemplifies the code of courtesy and its ultimate rejection through the depiction of character actions. The strongest points for argument are in the attempted seduction of Gawain by Bertilak's wife, and in the reaction to Gawain's expedition by Arthur at the end of the poem. First, Bertilak's wife attempts to seduce Gawain three times, but Gawain preserves his virtues and courtesy, while abandoning his duty to courtly love. In the third attempt, Gawain's obligations to Bertilak and to Bertilak's wife expose a flaw in courtesy and set up its rejection:

> Either take her tendered love or distastefully refuse.
> His courtesy concerned him, lest crass he appear,
> But more his soul's mischief, should he commit sin
> And belie his loyal oath to the lord of that house.
>
> ll. 1772–1774

Gawain is tied to the wife through courtly love and should fulfill her wishes; however, he is bound to her husband through courtesy, as well. He is concerned that he will appear insensitive to the woman, but he wants to preserve his virtues as a knight owing loyalty to his lord. Gawain must reject the strict code of courtesy to "retain both his honor and his reputation" (Markman, 584). He cannot fulfill the superficial mask of courtesy in both spheres, thus he must compromise to uphold his reputation and his virtues simultaneously. Gawain chooses to follow his virtues and maintain loyalty to his lord and attempts to fulfill his courtesy to the wife by accepting the girdle. However, accepting the girdle is his fall from perfect knighthood, as he conceals it from the lord intentionally. The acceptance of the girdle demonstrates that rejecting courtesy for one's own virtues (and Sir Gawain's life) should be acceptable within specific situations. After Gawain's fall and decision to keep the girdle, the Green Knight humbles him by exposing the deed that he committed at Bertilak's castle. Gawain returns to Arthur's court with newfound understanding of courtesy and the acceptance of being a humble knight. Upon his return, Gawain retells the adventures to Arthur and the court, yet "the king comforts the knight, and the court all together / Agree with great laughter" (ll. 2513–14). The end of the poem exposes the artificial nature of courtesy in the courts. The laughing of the court insinuates that they do not take genuineness seriously, rather they continue to accept the artificial mask of courtesy that Gawain now understands as incorrect. Arthur does not take the lesson seriously, even though Gawain understands the boasting of courtesy as "a sign of excess" (l. 2433). Gawain rejects traditional courtesy by refusing "to claim any glory when he returned to Arthur's court" (Markman, 577). Moreover, his resounding virtues and understanding of being genuine "informs all the virtues" that the Gawain-poet argues for in exchange for the current trend of proud knighthood and court behavior (586). These last lines of the poem fastidiously reject courtesy in a way that begs its readers to look for a more honest way to uphold courtesy without its interference in one's virtues.

The chivalric code, most importantly, courtesy is argued against throughout "Sir Gawain and the Green Knight" in a way that begs for society to address the flaws in such a utopic ideology. Courtesy beckons that people behave in a certain manner and follow certain codes to uphold a court's reputation. Sir Gawain follows his knightly code but finds that it does not harmoniously fit in with the courts expectations of men and women. He is to uphold his lord's reputation and have spectacular behavior even though it goes against his human nature and virtues. The Gawain-poet makes Gawain perfect for much of the poem, which sets him up for an ultimate fall that asserts that the idea of courtesy should be redefined as genuine behavior rather than a mask that hides the true actions and behaviors of a court. Hence, the poet's decision to paint Arthur in a prideful and arrogant light confirms that courtesy had been corrupted. By juxtaposing these two characters and using irony, figurative language, and actions, the poet successfully redefines and rejects the former version of knightly courtesy.

Male Control stripped by Female Identity

Eighteenth century literature largely exemplifies the damsel in distress and the man who saves her, but what does a piece of literature look like when female identity subjugates patriarchal hegemony? The poem "Adam Pos'd" by Anne Finch positions Adam in a postlapsarian state, or after the fall from the Garden of Eden. He is the man that labeled all-natural creatures including woman (Eve), but now faces a woman who expresses herself through fashion and cosmetics. The woman does not belong in the country setting that Finch places her in with Adam. The juxtaposition of the man who defined everything and a woman he cannot comprehend demonstrates the failures of patriarchy. The anachronism allows the poem to rise above the patriarchal themes of seventeenth and eighteenth century British literature that ridicule female behavior and grant her agency out of the reach of male control. Furthermore, the diction perverts gendered pronouns and gives a positive connotation to the word "Thing," as a woman's way of evading male-defined femininity. Anne Finch's poem "Adam Pos'd" uses irony and anachronism alongside biblical allusions to subjugate patriarchal hegemony within literature and liberate the female identity from the control of male-driven categorization.

    The biblical allusions are critical in understanding the method the poem uses to deconstruct patriarchy and establish the female identity external to conventions. For example, Adam is "at his toilsome Plough" with "Thorns in his Path" and "Cloth'd only in a rude unpolish'd Skin" (Finch, ll. 1–3). These lines allude to Genesis 3.18–23 in which the Bible describes Adam and his current setting after the fall from the Garden of Eden. He is depicted in despair, filthy, and living in a harsh setting unlike the period that Finch wrote in. Moreover, the reader can presume that the Adam in the title is indeed the Adam from the Bible, as he is referenced as "First Father" (l. 1). He is the man who defined the natural world. These biblical allusions juxtaposed against the modern woman presented in the poem set up the ability to see the irony of Adam unable to label the woman, thus shattering patriarchy and giving freedom to femininity.

Furthermore, the poem is built around irony and the careful word selection that satirizes patriarchal control over women. The poem ridicules female artificiality to present an argument against patriarchal hegemony. For example, Finch presents the woman as a "Fantastick Nymph" who is "in all her antick Graces" and in her "various Fashions" and "various Faces" (ll. 4–6). The words point out the ridiculousness of female superficiality. For example, according to the *Oxford English Dictionary*, "Fantastick" means either "imaginary or fabulous," while the word "antick" means "grotesque or figured with bizarre congruity." The words imply that the woman is adventurous, fanciful, and free from the traditional role of "wife" or "woman" as Adam understands her given definition. The ironic nature of these words suggests that this woman actively chooses to go against patriarchal tradition and flaunts it in Adam's presence. This describes the nature of an eighteenth-century coquette who has parted from the natural world for the sake of fashion and cosmetics.

    Finch is attempting to deconstruct female artificiality, yet the ironic tone lends to the subjugation of male control. For example, the title "Adam Pos'd" brings into question the capacity of male intellect with respect to women. The word "pos'd" means confused. It is odd that the "First Father" which is the epitome of patriarchy and the forefather of humankind would find himself perplexed by another creature. The tone begins to break down the grasp of male domination over female identity. Moreover, Adam knows that the nymph bears feminine qualities, as he chooses the pronoun "her," but he finds himself unable to label the woman. He cannot understand her changing faces and fashions. He cannot understand something that he has not named himself. Adam resorts to calling the woman an "it," and he is unable to "giv'n this Thing a Name" (ll. 7 and 11). The poet reveals that Adam cannot understand the unnaturalness of varying fashions and make-up with which the Nymph uses to express herself. He resorts to calling her by a non-gendered pronoun. This declassification of the woman by Adam releases the female identity from the grasp of male rationality. Ultimately, femininity triumphs the masculine control often seen in literature; her agency is not defined by hard-working Adam.

The ironic nature of the poem and the diction are useful to the destruction of patriarchal hegemony, but it is the anachronistic placement of the nymph in Adam's world that truly liberates female identity from the control of men. The woman in the poem is not from the same time period as Adam, as can be argued by the nature of her dress. After Adam evaluates the woman's attire and makeup for which he cannot understand, he concludes, "[a] guest from what New Element she came which illustrates that she is not of the natural setting that he" is accustomed to (l. 10). The nymph does not belong to the natural world that Adam knows, thus her misplacement confuses him and prevents him from controlling her label. The nymph lies outside of his scope of control. The insertion of an eighteenth-century woman into the postlapsarian setting remove man's ability to categorize and oppress women into a predefined mold. Furthermore, the anachronistic placement of Adam and the Nymph allows Finch to play with the man's capacity for understanding woman and ultimately allows her to subjugate patriarchy. Adam cannot define the woman because she did not exist in the Garden of Eden, where he was in control of categorization of all creatures. She does not need him to define her, as she has defined herself; Finch empowers femininity and gives it a name that cannot be controlled by male-centric society.

Anne Finch plays with irony and diction to mold a poem into a powerful feminine statement, while turning patriarchy in on itself. Merging the modern woman alongside postlapsarian Adam permits the argument of female identity existing outside of patriarchal hegemony to be born. She is undefinable to the first man on earth, thus patriarchal domination has no grasp on the birth of female identity and agency. Moreover, while Finch satirizes female artificiality, she does so in a light-hearted manner that sets up the downfall of man's capacity to understand what he has not defined. At the end of the poem, the speaker calls the woman a "Thing," which could be read as oppressing female agency, yet it is the fact that Adam cannot define her that makes being a "Thing" positive. Being undefinable by the source of oppression is more powerful than being allowed agency under the house of patriarchy.

Explication Anne Finch's "Adam Pos'd"

Anne Finch's poem, "Adam Pos'd" uses specific context and language to create a scene to juxtapose the male perspective against the female being. The biblical allusions are striking throughout the poem, but the most striking is the postlapsarian position of Adam. He is "at his toilsome Plough" and "Cloth'd only in a rude, unpolish'd Skin" (ll. 2–3). This is an allusion to Genesis 3.18–23, in which the Bible describes Adam after the fall from Eden. He is at his lowest point in his life, having failed God. The postlapsarian position is critical to the entire poem, as it means that Adam has already met Eve and has already named/defined everything in the world. Hence, when the reader discovers that Adam cannot understand the Nymph, the theme of female identity and patriarchy surface.

By presenting the reader with an already fallen Adam, we know that he has met Eve, thus this is not the first time that he has encountered a feminine creature. He is not confused about her feminine nature; rather he cannot understand her changing faces and fashions. He cannot understand something that he has not named under God's will. For example, the speaker positions the line "Her various fashions and more various faces" in the presence of the words "Thing" and "it" (ll. 6, 7, and 11). The poet shows that Adam cannot understand the unnaturalness of varying fashions and make-up with which the Nymph expresses herself. After this line, the reader sees a direct shift in Adam's perspective of the woman. He calls her "it" and cannot believe that she has the "Skill" to transform herself in front of him. By the end of the poem, he is astonished and decides that the "Thing" is something so out of reach that he cannot give it a name.

Additionally, the word choice within the spectrum of Adam being placed after the fall provides the argument that the female figure cannot be controlled or categorized by the male perspective (or perhaps control). The speaker uses the word "Fantastick" to describe the Nymph (l. 4). The word suggests the woman is adventurous, fanciful, and most importantly, not dutiful, as the biblical wife is expected to be. This woman abandons the rules and expresses the "dirty" side that Eve was punished for, though she does it in front of the man that fell from Eve's actions. The woman is free from patriarchy and will do as she pleases, even if that means she exists outside of the control of man or of society.

Fame and Fortune, Lives' Forgotten: Thomas Gray's "Elegy Written in a Country Churchyard

Thomas Gray's "Elegy Written in a Country Churchyard" reflects on the lives' of humble villagers buried in a country cemetery while commenting on the inevitability of death for all people regardless of social class. The speaker positions "The short and simple annals of the poor" (32) alongside "The paths of glory lead but to the grave" (36) to show that fortune and fame cannot save anybody from being forgotten after the event of their death, nor does death value one person's life over another person's life. Additionally, through the juxtaposition of the imagery of the lives of the rich and poor Gray argues that the unhonored dead could have been important in life had they been given the same opportunities as the rich.

Gray utilizes personification to emphasize that death does not spare the upper class, and to highlight that the lives of the people without lavish gravestones were as valuable as the rich who could afford gravestones. The poem opens with, "The Curfew tolls the knell of parting day," which personifies "Curfew" as the transitional being that separates life from death (1). By personifying "Curfew" Gray implies that the transition from life to death is a set element assigned to all people regardless of social class; furthermore, the word "curfew" suggests a constant, daily segment of every day that occurs as the world keeps moving beyond those who have already met their curfew. The tone of this "Curfew" is established with the word "knell," which is a mournful sound, thus implying that the curfew is not one that brings life. Additionally, Gray personifies the attitudes of the upper class to illustrate that the lives of the hard-working villagers are as worthy as the lives of the rich. For example, the speaker says,

> Let not Ambition mock their useful toil
> Their homely joys, and destiny obscure;

> Nor Grandeur hear with a disdainful smile
> The short and simple annals of the poor. (29–32).

Gray personifies "Ambition" to state that the poor should not allow the rich to degrade the simple enjoyments that they have in life (29). This presents the idea that one's life need not be full of grandiose goals in order to be a valuable citizen, nor does ambitious nature to seek fortune prevent death from coming at one's curfew. Moreover, "Grandeur" is personified to stand in as the haughty attitudes of those that are of great importance whilst living (31). The juxtaposition of "Grandeur" (31) with the "short and simple" (32) lives of countrymen illustrates that the opinions of the upper class are not important and that their stories will be just as forgotten as those with large amounts of wealth. Gray dismantles the social classes by rejecting the concept that great people will be more remembered than those who did not have the wealth to construct elaborate headstones.

The metaphors throughout the poem allow Gray to propose that the unhonored dead could have had similar opportunities as the rich if social class did not exist, and that in death everybody becomes equal. First, death equalizes everybody's position in life as Gray compares all of the graves to a "narrow cell" in which the "rude forefathers sleep," and these two lines do not alter the state of the grave nor distinguish between the poor or the rich (15–16). Thereby, Gray succeeds in demonstrating that all of the dead are buried in the same sized plots and there is nothing that can distinguish one ancestor from the other. While much of the imagery in the poem is geared toward death as the great equalizer, he provides imagery that suggests that the poor also die with missed opportunities. In stanza fourteen Gray writes,

> Full many a gem of purest ray serene
> The dark unfathm'd caves of ocean bear,
> Full many a flower is born to blush unseen.

>And waste its sweetness on the desert air (53–56).

Gray compare the villagers to lost gems in the ocean and budding flowers in the desert that never get to be smelled, which positions the poor as folks with talent, but they lack the resources to succeed in those talents before they die. One could relate the gems and flowers to all people that go through life unappreciated, since the speaker says, "Th' applause of list'ning senates" (61) is not granted to poor folks' good deeds due to their social status. In the aforementioned metaphor, Gray emphasizes the unfortunate loss of potential due to social class through anaphora, "Full many a" (53 and 55). The anaphora within the metaphor suggests that too many poor die without the opportunity or recognition of contributing to society.

The contrasting imagery between the rich and the poor's gravestones in the churchyard exemplify the concepts that the poor die with missed opportunities, and that fame and fortune do not allow the rich to evade death. Constantly, Gray raises the question as to whether one is remembered after death. The speaker asks of the rich, "Can storied urn or animated bust / Can honour's voice provoke the silent dust / Or flattery soothe the dull cold ear of death?" (41–44). This quote points out that once the soul dies there are no words, epitaphs, or headstones that can realign the body with the soul, thus there is no guarantee that one's life will be remembered since eventually everybody will die. He then compares the rich's burying rituals to that of the poor, "Their names, their years, spelt by th' unletter'd muse" (81) to highlight that the simplicity of these gravestones will render the same effect as the elaborate gravestones of the rich. The paralleling of the imagery argues that the wealth and fame earned during life will have no bearing on the future one has after death. Again, Gray inserts anaphors to emphasize the relationships between the rich and the poor that are so distant, yet so close within the precept of death. Furthermore, Gray continues to address the lower class's missed opportunities as he reflects upon the gravestones. In stanza twelve, the speaker imagines what the poor could have become had their fates been different while they were still alive:

> Perhaps in this neglected spot is laid
> Some heart once pregnant with celestial fire;
> Hands, that the rod of empire might have sway'd,
> Or wak'd to ecstasy the living lyre (45–48).

The speaker speculates that the unkempt gravestone of this poor person could have become a great scholar, king, or musician had he been given the chance to do so within his lifetime. Unfortunately, this is another somber moment in the poem where the tone married with the imagery gives Gray the chance to argue that social class in life deters all of society from becoming the people that they want to become, by stating that the poor man was "pregnant" with a passion befitting for the gods. The poem is the opportunity for the unappreciated and underrepresented poor to have a remembered position in society.

Thomas Gray's "Elegy Written in a Country Churchyard" is an exemplary poem that uses a number of literary devices to demonstrate many themes and representations of death between social classes. The use of metaphor, personification, and figurative imagery give Gray the opportunities to propose that the poor are unhonored for their contributions to society, that social class prevents people from achieving their full potential before death knocks at the door, and that neither fame nor fortune can save a person from the event of death (or of people forgetting that they ever lived).

Gwendolyn Brooks' "The Mother": Maternal Ambivalence and Agency in Non-Traditional Mothers

Societal constructs argue that abortion does not grant motherhood, but is that so? Can a woman become a mother in the choice of abortion? This ideology is being pushed against by critics such as Elizabeth Podnieks and Andrea O'Reilly in the chapter "Maternal Literatures in Text and Tradition: Daughter-Centric, Matrilineal, and Matrifocal Perspectives," in which the elements of what make a mother become present in women who have had children and those who have not. Two elements apply directly toward a woman who has had an abortion: maternal agency and maternal ambivalence. Maternal ambivalence refers to a mother who feels positive and negative emotions toward her children, while maternal agency refers to a mother who chooses her own autonomy and desires over her children. The concepts of maternal ambivalence and agency are present in Gwendolyn Brooks' poem "The Mother," which takes the perspective of a woman who has aborted her children yet struggles with the feelings of motherhood in the aftermath. The speaker of "The Mother" establishes maternal agency and maternal ambivalence through diction, tone, and the juxtaposition of imagery and ideas, which allows the speaker to empower herself as a mother in spite of choosing abortion over child rearing.

The empathetic, yet apathetic tone in "The Mother" highlights maternal ambivalence, allowing the speaker to grant agency to her and all women in the face of raising children. Maternal ambivalence is clear in "The Mother" as the speaker struggles with being a mother of aborted children; she is not remorseful of her choice, yet it is clear that she loves her unborn children. For example, the speaker states, "The damp small pulps with a little or no hair," and then proceeds to state, "The singers and workers that never handled the air" in regard to these lifeless beings (ll. 3–4). The speaker refers to them as pulps, but then she fantasizes about what their lives would have been had she kept them. All mothers dream of what their children will do with their lives, but many do not picture them as pulps. By creating the duality of love and indifference, the tone magnifies the "unattainable image of motherhood" and demonstrates that she can love these unborn children as much dead as if they would have been alive (10). The tone seeks to "unmask motherhood" and break down the "cultural expectations [that] demand that a mother love her child unconditionally" (17). She remains authentic to her feelings as a mother and unveils to society that mothers experience complex emotions simultaneously towards their children. By doing so, she demonstrates her alignment and indifference towards the children; thus, she is breaking the construct of who is entitled to motherhood and the array of feelings that encompass motherhood.

While the tone establishes maternal ambivalence, the juxtaposition of imagery and ideas illustrates the speaker's maternal agency. The speaker chooses to have abortions for personal reasons and her desire to protect her children. The first stanza highlights the juxtaposition and agency, "You will never neglect or beat / Them, or silence or buy with a sweet / Or scuttle off ghosts that come. / You will never leave them" (ll. 5, 6, 8, and 9). By putting these images together, she paints a picture of real motherhood, rather than portraying an ideal motherhood that does not exist. These negative images married to the positive images show that the mother is protecting her children from the evils of her world, even if that means she must sacrifice the heart-warming experience she would have while raising the children. Not only does she assert that abortion was the best choice for her children, she "implements a mode of mothering that mitigates the many ways that patriarchal motherhood … regulates and restrains mothers" (l. 17). The alternative "mode of mothering" grants her motherhood in a discourse that shames women for stepping outside of the societal expectations of a mother. The speaker becomes a mother and possesses agency of her motherhood. Another juxtaposition that shows maternal agency is between the title, "The Mother" and line 1, "Abortions will not let you forget" (1). Podnieks and O'Reilly would claim that this is "real maternal agency" and it "enables [mothers] to face and resist ... the pressure of other people's policing of their mothering" (18). As society does not consider a woman who aborts a child a mother, the proximity between the two words marks the woman's belief that she is a mother and the choice of abortion was a maternal decision. The claim that a woman can have an abortion and still be a mother demonstrates agency because the mother is challenging the common discourse of motherhood.

The diction in "The Mother" grants the speaker motherhood by expressing maternal agency and ambivalence. Word choice and connotation influence the feelings behind the speaker's thoughts on her aborted children as she remembers her decisions. Word choice is important to the maternal discourse as the speaker demonstrates maternal ambivalence through her inability to label the aborted fetuses. The speaker progresses from "children" to "dears" to "Sweets" as she seeks to explain her motherly choices (ll. 11, 14, and 15). This progression exemplifies the "complex and contradictory" mindset that women feel toward their children (Podneiks and O'Reilly, 16). These wavering feelings are the love and hate that a woman may feel towards her children because she cannot settle with herself on the abortions, and the maternal nature presents itself in her choice to give them a pet name. She empowers herself as a mother by calling them a name that a mother would call her living children, thereby shattering the idea that only true mothers can feel maternal. Likewise, maternal agency becomes apparent in the connotation of several words used within the narrative. For example, the speaker empowers herself as a mother by stating, "Believe that even in my *deliberateness*, I was not *deliberate*." (l. 23, emphasis added). The noun "deliberateness" could mean the quality or amount of being deliberate, which suggests that the speaker was aware of her actions, or that her deliberation was of sound mind. On the other hand, the adjective "deliberate" paired with "not" means that she did not take a lot of time to make the decision. Thereby the speaker is telling her children that she made the choice, but she did not do it with malice. The woman honors her choice as a mother and does not let society make her "feel guilty [about her] experiences of mothering" (10). Remaining authentic to her perspective of motherhood challenges the societal ideology of motherhood and permits all women who fall outside of the typical definition to claim motherhood.

Motherhood is not dichotomous. Women can become mothers through a multitude of ways, including abortion. Gwendolyn Brooks' wrote "The Mother" before society was ready to hear about the idea that a woman who has aborted her children experiences maternal agency and maternal ambivalence in the aftermath of the decision (even today, we are not ready for this conversation). Through a number of successful literary devices, the poem's speaker establishes herself as a mother who made a decision based on her need and the needs of her children. She expresses ambivalence in her diction and tone in her inability to demonstrate just one feeling towards the decision. Her love for her children is understandable by any mother, as is her indifference towards their lack of being. Moreover, her ability to establish agency through diction and juxtaposition situates the door into traditional motherhood discourse to sway in a new direction. Even in the success of this poem's skill in pressing against the perception of motherhood, the discussion leaves many questions about empowerment within motherhood and the redefinition of being a mother. What does it really take to become a mother?

On CA Conrad's "How the Fuck Do I Get Out of this Place"

The tone, diction, and punctuation of CA Conrad's "How the Fuck Do I Get Out of this Place" contribute to my reading of a poem that examines, or perhaps questions, gender fluidity and social singularities.

The tone of the poem is a combination of a saddened honesty and sarcasm. The start of the poem begins with, "no I cannot win a knife fight," which feels vulnerable and honest. The word choice and sentence structure convey this attitude. The first word is 'no' and that seems to be a response from the speaker to an authority figure, or of a question positioned in a way that only leaves one answer; it limits the possibilities. Combine "no" with the word "cannot" that follows, and the lines quickly takes a sad turn, as it becomes an admission of defeat. Through the word "cannot," the speaker confers this as fact and there is no changing it. The rigidity presented in this statement lends to the feeling of the speaker feeling alone in a society that does not welcome both the idea of a yes and a no existing simultaneously, which thus lends to the overall gender fluidity presented throughout Conrad's poetry. However, while the first line is depressingly honest, Conrad is quick to insert humor and sarcasm in the very next line with, "for the fifteenth time" and complexes the meaning of line one. Sarcasm and humor add a line of defense to the speaker; he may have successfully won fourteen knife fights, but the question arises, why was he involved in so many knife fights? The tone continuum moves back and forth from line to line, so much so that it becomes difficult to know exactly what is going on in the poem, but I believe that is the point of the poem.

    This rolling together of lines adds another complexity to the poem: multiple potential readings depending the reader's innate placement of breaths and pauses. The multiple readings occur due to the omission of punctuation and radical enjambment. For example, lines 1–4 offer a variety of readings due to the enjambment and reader's choice to insert punctuation/pauses. The lines read, "no I cannot win a knife fight /

for the fifteenth time / I didn't see who / stabbed him." At first, I read lines 1–2 as the speaker being unable to win a knife fight again, but during my second evaluation of the lines, I read line one alone and lines 2–3 together, which positioned the speaker as being questioned about witnessing a crime. By inserting a comma at the end of line one, and subsequently reading lines 2–3 together, it altered the speaker's role. The speaker is no longer an active participant in the knife fight; rather, he is in the line of questioning as a witness (and perhaps involved). Becoming the witness allows the speaker to see what the authority figure and the knife fight participants cannot see in the world, which speaks to the overall theme of being an outlier on a designated spectrum. Multiple readings are seen in "earache could be / from hearing / your last words / over and over in dreams" as well. If lines 16 and 17 are read together with a natural pause placed at the end of line 17, then the speaker is in pain from hearing the "your" utter his/her last words. On the other hand, if I read the work straight through line 18, then I am subjected to the speaker's dream world.

The layering of meaning that Conrad performs through enjambment and punctuation permits the reader to become a direct participant in the meaning of the poem; the reader adds natural pauses and derives different meanings based on how the lines are read together.

Conrad's poem begs to be read multiple ways with a subtle ear to pick up on the oscillating tone and themes he explores through enjambment and the lack of punctuation.

The New Boys

In Mei-Mei Berssenbrugge's poem "The New Boys," the ambiguous tone develops through excessive pronoun use and diction. I question further if her choice to combine a specific register of words with singular and plural pronouns is a statement of her poetics, of her collage style that perhaps is "unformed."

The ambiguous tone first develops in the string of singular and plural male pronouns. From section to section, we have subtle transformations in the use of the pronouns. Section One is entirely singular, Section Two is a rich combination of singular and plural, while Section Three slowly moves back from the plural to singular usage. Another technique to point out is the development of the "I" from section one to section three. Section One uses very little "I," and by the time we reach the end of Section Three the use of "I" is much more prevalent. But let's return to the male pronouns. Given the title, "The New

Boys" suggests multiple boys or a group of boys alongside the ambiguous use of "he," "him," and "his" throughout the poem (particularly in section one), it becomes unclear if the pronouns represent multiple men or different versions of the same man. After much consideration, I believe that the singular male pronouns stand in for different men that the speaker has been in contact with, but they are wrapped up into the one man she is currently interacting with. Why? There is a lot of action done by the he/his/him in section one. For example, the speaker writes, "He says," "His thoughts dissolve," "He has no need," "His comprehension is," "he tries," and "he relates," which are used to describe what the man is doing or thinking, or how the speaker perceives the man during their conversation in the café. In every instance that man does something, what is being done is muddled by an unformed or abstract notion/act. Berssenbrugge combines the pronouns with "extraterrestrials," "mistiness," and "chaos". Moreover, the speaker says, "I'm trying to stabilize what he says with respect to a line of meaning, one word after another, but he's sensitive and the words are turbulent." The speaker tried to make meaning of the man's words and actions, but she is unable to do so. It becomes unclear to me and, I think, the speaker as to who it is that she is with. That ambiguity speaks to the notion of a multitude of men, which the speaker alludes to in the last stanza of Section One saying, "but I speak of it obliquely as young men and possibilities I imagine for romance." The ambiguous tone is a platform for the continuum (or perhaps multitude or multiplicity) of men the speaker has interacted with.

    The singular pronoun we see in Section One morphs into plural and singular pronouns in Sections Two and Three. Berssenbrugge writes, "In triple layers of jackets, they look so slender," as well as, "My overall impression of him is composed of moment to moment sensation as connection." In the first line here, "they" potentially coincides with the group of boys previously mentioned placed into multiple jackets, yet still looking slender. The image is unclear since most men would look thick should they be wearing multiple jackets. Do the jackets serve to mask the boys? To cover up the interiority that the speaker has yet to reveal about the "they" and the "he" we have seen so far? Or, is this how the speaker views men, in a haze? Then we have the second line, more personal because the "I" has come forward to say that the man is only visible in brief snippets, never as a whole, but strung together. It is ambiguous, the tone of the lines and the image of man. What is a man to the speaker? Is man a collage of all experiences with men? At this point, we still have not seen a clear image of the man she is with outside of brief mentions of artistry and "unformed" perceptions. Even at the mention of the man named Soko, who the speaker met online, the speaker still resigns to tell us that she read about his friends too. A singular interest is not present. I noted that it does not seem as though the singular male pronouns are void of connection, nor does it seem that Berssenbrugge is trying to confuse the reader, rather the ambiguous tone and language are a tool to establish the speaker's connection to both man and men in a collage technique. And perhaps this collaging of singular and plural represents the speaker's relationship with men, maleness, and/or masculinity, regardless of how fumbling it is. To be "unformed" does not necessarily speak to being unaware or ambivalent as one might presume at the forefront, rather, it is to say that nothing, whether that be the speaker, the poetry, or the subject, has one particular form. In essence, ambiguity.

Cole Swensen's Gravesend

Alliteration and anaphora in the poem "Sometimes the Ghost" by Cole Swensen guided my reading of the piece.

The power of the poem rests with the sounds and the rhythm developed through alliteration. Starting with line one of the prose poem, a domino effect, or perhaps a weaving technique begins to happen as the alliteration of one hard consonant is dropped for another. For example, Swensen starts the poem with 's' sounds in the words "Sometimes" and "arrives," before dropping the 's' in exchange for a series of hard 'b' words: "before," "body," and "breath." This alliterative pattern continues with 'w' sounds ("which," "will," "white," "will," and "walls"), and again with 'c' sounds ("cause," "cause," and "crawl"). Upon the introduction of the 'w' sounds, we see Swensen subtly begin to drop and pick up previously used consonants, much like crochet stiches. The sounds resurface and drop creating a sonic rhythm in a similar fashion to Gertrude Stein's work. By creating a standard acoustic sound throughout the poem, not only does a haunting rhythm develop, but it also illuminates the ghost traveling throughout the poem. The alliteration allows the word "ghost" to become a prominent and surprisingly illusive fixture. The word itself appears three times, and each time it reads as if I've read it for the first time. The ghost, both the word and the apparition, come in and out of visibility the way I would imagine an actual ghost moving in and out of the conscious world. This movement mirrors the speaker's state of being as the ghost moves from the body of the other into the space around it and back in again.

Through diction and phrasing, the tone of the poem is haunting. Moreover, the word choice leads to confusion as to who the actual ghost is in the poem. First, in line one, the phrase "before the body is gone" sets up an out-of-body feeling that resonates throughout the rest of the poem. The eerie tone stems from the fact that the phrase is in reference to the ghost, an entity in culture that surfaces after the body has left the physical realm and not while the body is still present. And then the speaker says, "and cause the ghost to crawl up inside … and the ghost walks around looking like you" (ll. 3–4). Here the speaker infers that the ghost was exterior to the body, but something causes it to enter the body and become the operating mechanism. Moreover, it would seem that this takeover removes the previous self in exchange for a being on autopilot, all of which lends to the haunting tone. This notion leads me to ask several questions. Does this mean that the ghost holds the body in motion while the spirit and physical being ready for its final exit? How fluid are the realms of being that allow the ghost to move inward and outward? Lines three and four are scary, as they imply that the ghost may have more agency than the physical being, but I feel that they set up the confusion at the end of the poem. And by confusion, I am referring to a muddling of who is who. The final sentence of the poem, "And I walk across the room with my eyes closed," leaves me wondering if the speaker is in fact communicating with her ghost. The phrase "eyes closed" allows me to draw this conclusion because of the previous reference to eyes failing in line four. If the body loses its sight as the ghost takes over, then is the admission that the speaker is indeed the ghost? Or is the speaker walking away from its ghost? Or was it another's ghost. Many of these questions are unanswered, but they seal the haunting tone that began so early in the poem. Ultimately, it allows the question of agency and other to develop, leading to the idea that we never truly know if we are the ghost or if we are the physical being.

Harryette Mullen's
S*p*rm**k*t

Harryette Mullen's poem "Just add water..." makes uses of diction to expose themes of domestication and consumerism in connection to the woman.

The poem, like the others in this collection, examines the language and construction of the supermarket as it relates to women (or perhaps, as it relates to the social construction of domestic roles). The word choice is to expose the argument Mullen makes about consumerism and women in a domestic setting. For example, the first two sentences, "Just add water. That homespun incantation activates potent powders, alchemical concentrates, jars and boxes of abracadabra," immediately draw our attention to consumption, but more importantly to the construction of modern domesticity. First, the phrase "just add water" is commonly listed on products such as pancake mix, cake mixes, and condensed soups at the store. What do all of these things have in common with one another?

Water. Water is the basic necessity of life and is now a magic tool. Water simplifies the domestic sphere, or at least convinces the consumer that she can still be a homemaker without losing her agency. By allowing the woman to feel as if she can still be a "proper woman", consumerism has successfully maintained the construction of domestication, with women at home and men out of the home. All with a little bit of magic. Mullen's choice of words lends to that notion. She uses the phrases "homespun incantation" and "abracadabra." According to the *Oxford English Dictionary*, "incantation" is magical spell or charm that produces a magical effect on the sorcerer and those around her. Combine that with homespun and Mullen evokes the domestic sphere controlled by consumerism. Women can perform magic at home with certain products. In this way, Mullen shows that women's roles in domesticity are constructed through product advertisement; it gives women choices that seem like freeing solutions, but really they are simply a magical spell to mediate women.

The poem further contributes to the construction and containment of women in a domestic role through consumerism in the lines about bottled water. Mullen compares bottled water to tap water in a way that makes the packaged goods more desirable than the water that streams from the faucet. Mullen describes bottled water as "clearly miracle H-2-0" that is "cleaner than North Pole snow" and "purer than ... drops distilled from sterile virgin tears." Alternatively, Mullen pens tap water as "municipal precipitate." The adjustment in the register of the diction highlights the way products are sold in comparison to something more natural (even though I'd argue that tap water is treated much like a consumer product in our society). The bottled water is made beautiful; it is spruced up and marketed to women as better than the free, wild version, and thus constructing the idea that a packaged item is better than the same item in its original state. By writing water in two different forms, Mullen exposes the societal construction of women as products, as objects or beings that are better off packaged and beautiful rather than in a natural state. The argument that this constructs the domestic roles of women could be extended to include the physical female body too. Moreover, Mullen writes bottled water as purer than a virgin's tears. It makes me question if the idea of purity becomes more important than purity itself. Does a woman presenting purity become more marketable than a woman who presents her body as it is, pure or impure? History would say that the construction of virginity, of purity of the female body is more important. What does the water metaphor say about the boundaries of the female body? Of its physical presentation?

Claudia Rankine's Citizen

To better understand thread of exclusion and inclusion, or perhaps spoken versus unspoken thread throughout Claudia Rankine's poetry, I examined the tone and "you" in the vignette that begins with, "Standing outside the conference room" (50).

Before I discuss the tone, and particularly the language within the poem that leads me to my thoughts, I want to touch on how the subjective nature of the address both invites and excludes the reader as the speaker navigates the event. First, in this vignette, the speaker overhears two men discussing their inability to understand black people when they communicate. The speaker is unseen by the two men, and after the men finish the conversation, the speaker waits a moment before entering the conference room, where she is a member of the meeting about to take place. As a reader, I am invited to feel the discomfort that this overhearing causes, and yet I cannot fully grasp the speaker's reaction to the moment because we lack the common thread that caused the conversation between the men, skin color. And that notion is what makes the "you" so powerful in the poetry. By excluding the reader this way, the power of the exclusion on the subjective becomes more tangible; the speaker allows the reader to really sense the struggle of navigating a society that is supposed to welcome the speaker in, but still pushes the speaker to the outskirts. The "you" is never included in the "we," or other that is outlined in the poem. The dichotomy further enhances the speaker's choice to be heard or to be silent during these events.

How does the tone and "you" of this vignette demonstrate inclusion/exclusion and spoken/unspoken? First, I would note that the tone is uncomfortable and wry. The speaker is "unseen" by the two men that are speaking about black people being incomprehensible. Since, I have concluded that the speaker includes herself in that category, the entire poem becomes uncomfortable. The speaker hides and waits for the men to stop speaking about it. The topic of the conversation puts the speaker in an awkward position; she feels that she must "wait … before entering the room" to avoid making the men feel uncomfortable. In this gesture, the speaker bears all of the situation's awkwardness, and does not make the men feel ashamed/guilty for what they have just said. Not only is the speaker subjected to the terrible interaction between these men, she must now pretend as though she did not hear it. Or at least she chooses to give them that freedom. What does that say about the speaker's relationship with society? By choosing not to speak, is that her forgiving society for its prejudiced beliefs about the black community? Or would she rather be "unseen" to avoid unnecessary confrontation about the racist remarks? I am unsure, but I do think that this poem highlights how the speaker is both included in society, but she is treated as the rule, not the exception. We see these choices unfolding in the internal dialogue of the you, as the you "hears" and "will spend" and "considers" the ramifications in speaking out. The uncomfortable tone is often made a tad funny with Rankine's delicately executed wry tone. For example, one of the men tells the other man that "being around black people is like watching a foreign film without translation," which is not funny at all. In fact, it is quite terrible. What makes the tone wry is the context of the statement. We know that the speaker speaks English, and we know that most African American communities speak English, and yet this man is saying black people speaking English is akin to a foreign language. The gravity of the statement is offset by its absurdity. Further wryness occurs when the speaker says, "around the round table that makes conversing easier." This statement comes after the men claim that black people cannot be understood. The round table is a subtle stab at the lack of inclusion of the speaker in the communication about to take place at the meeting. Since the speaker now knows that these men will not hear what she has to say, the point of a table inviting all to participate in the conversation is useless. I would note too, that the tone surrounding the round table becomes even funnier when we take into account the history of that table, and the Arthurian legends. The round table in Arthurian tales was a place solely for knights who were men and considered highly noble. Women and those who were not knights were not welcome at this table.

Charles Bernstein's Recalculating

Charles Bernstein's poem "Prose" is a reflection on poetry as an art form. The poem addresses a poem as a "worthless" commodity that cannot be bartered with or sold the same way that movies, paintings, or songs can be sold. Through tone and diction, I see Bernstein not only evaluating the worth of poetry, but also the importance of language. Poetry, much like language, is priceless.

While the tone is ominously dark and humorous, I suspect that there is also a triumphant (perhaps a slight push toward the humorous) tone existing as a sublayer. Before I touch on this triumphant "poetry is better" tone, let's hone in on the dark tone throughout the poem. The entire poem, with the exception of the last sentence and a few phrases, works to undercut the value of poetry, or at the very least to render a poem priceless. The dark tone surfaces when Bernstein explains that poems "can't be sold like junk" and insinuates that these things can be sold for more. Is this a pointed argument about consumerism? About the consumption of commodities? Or is this a sad statement about the respect our society has for poetry? None of the above, or all? Regardless of Bernstein's true meaning, there is something dark about placing a poem below the selling value of junk. Or that paintings, prose, songs, "vats of burnt oil," and "graffiti" can warrant a value, but poems cannot. Both vats of burnt oil and graffiti are generally considered to be societal problems, not sources of commodity/art. This scaffolding of words, from traditional artwork to non-traditional forms of art and of course non-art, creates the dark tone. Even the last line, which I consider to be hilarious and an inside joke on poetry actually being priceless as a positive factor, can be skewed as negative. The poet calls himself a "lousy trader in worthless things," which is depressing, but ultimately seals my argument on the triumphant undertone that I read throughout the poem. The poet seems to be calling himself lousy at trading the poems, but he is not saying that he is bad at what he does. In fact, I think there is a sly displacement going on here, as if the poet is telling the rest of the world to keep walking, do not try this at home. Not to mention, the word "worthless" is grimmer than the word priceless. Where does the triumphant tone begin? The very first words of the poem, "A poem can't be sold," implies that everything else can, and, when something can be sold or value can be placed upon it, it has the opportunity to depreciate in value. Thus, a poem never depreciates, while everything else sold as art does. Bernstein further solidifies this tone with the phrase, "a poem don't live beyond its words." Here the tone is sly; Bernstein is making fun of art. More importantly, Bernstein is saying that language, that poetry does not need anything more than language. It simply exists as it is, without the validation of being purchased, unlike a painting that may wither with time. The grammatical choice here also implies something sarcastic about the speaker's tone towards language in poetry. The choice to make a grammatical error highlights the aesthetics of language and how intimate one becomes with language, the same way that readers become intimate with a poem. Lastly, poetry is elevated in a sphere of its own peaks at "beset by a plague of words," which ends the poem. A plague is unavoidable; a disease or oncoming of something that attacks its subject. The absurdity (hilarity?) sets poetry and language as unavoidable; language is more intimate than selling anything.

Hello, the Roses

Mei-Mei Berssenbrugge's poem "Hello, the Roses" is a language-rich poem combining both the physical with the intellectual. A connection between woman and flower comes alive in this poem, but what pulled me in the most about this poem was the execution of alliteration and other sonic elements that connected the lines together even when I was not sure what to make of them.

My first fascination with this poem was the consistent employment of alliteration and assonance. Each stanza holds its own sound pattern, butthere are also certain alliteration patterns that provide linkage throughout the poem. The sounds that we hear repeating throughout the poem are hard 'c,' 'b,' and 'r,' as well as the soft 's' sound. The connections allow for associations to be made. For example, the word 'color' is repeated throughout the poem as the speaker moves through various roses and explications of vision. Likewise, each stanza holds its own sonic patterns. For example, in stanza one, Berssenbrugge writes, "edges of my body, according to the same laws / by which stars shine, communicating with my body by emanation." The strongest alliteration occurs with "body…by…body" and "soul…same…stars…shine." The unfolding of the 's' and 'b' sounds, develop a sonic rhythm within this stanza, but also these sounds come back throughout the remainder of the poem. It reminds me of the movement of waves as they rise and fall. The oscillation of soft 's' and hard 'b' create a melody and the sounds harken back to the phrase, "My soul radially whorls out to the edges" in that the sounds in this stanza function like ripples in the water, moving the soul to the edges. Other stanzas that maintained an individual sound pattern include stanzas five, ten, and twenty. Stanza five marries a combination of hard 'r' sounds with the assonances of 'o' and 'e' to create a melody. Berssenbrugge tethers together "rose…records…recall" with "entire . . . emotion . . . emotion," and through these strings of words the 'o' sounds come through too. Unlike stanza one, the sonic movement in this stanza works to slow the rhythm down, rather than oscillate like ripples, these sounds feel as if they are slowly unfolding the language as the speaker further enhances the relationship with the rose. The lines remind me of time-lapsed photography revealing the slow blossoming of a rose. Slowing down the rhythm allows the reader to visualize this rose opening its petals, releasing the aroma and develop an emotional thread to the beauty of the soul and its ever-expanding reach into the world (which I believe the poet touches on in the first stanza). Lastly, stanza twenty relies on assonance to develop rhythm and an internal rhyme. In the stanza, Berssenbrugge writes, "the garden glows with a quality of light I might see when light shines through mist or in early morning." Instantly, I notice the alliteration of "garden" and "glows," as well as "mist" and "morning," both alliterations that establish a sonic meter in which the first word is hard and the final word in the pattern is soft. I was surprised to see the internal rhyme of might/light/light in a poem that executed sonic techniques so smoothly, but upon second look, it was a break from her standard rhythm. What exactly was the point of this, I am unsure, but something important seems to be said here with repetition of the word 'light' since Berssenbrugge is concerned with light throughout the poem. But, what I do notice is that through this exacting rhyme is the memory of others points in the poem where she refers to the word light or to qualities of seeing, which requires light.

On Prose

Wolf-Alice: Mirrors, Menstruation, and Language

The Gothic re-scripting of the Red Riding Hood fairytale in Angela Carter's *Wolf-Alice* begs the reader to understand the importance of balance between humanity and beastliness. *Wolf-Alice* tells the story of Wolf-Alice, a girl raised by wolves, abandoned by nuns, and left to come of age and discover her identity in the blood chamber of a man who is in the liminal space between man and beast. The story focuses on the Wolf-Alice's maturation in her own liminal space and how she becomes human through her sexuality and recognition of her self-image. Wolf-Alice experiences a transformation from animal-objectivity to human-subjectivity through the start of menstruation and recognizing herself in the mirror. Her sexual maturation gives her the concept of time and empowers her, as external forces do not subjugate her (her animal instincts remain intact). Her recognition in the mirror is similar to that of Lacan's mirror stage, in which one first believes that it is another person and then realizes that it is merely a reflection. According to Lacan's theory, once a person recognizes the reflection, there is a fragmentation between the body and the ego. However, Wolf-Alice does not experience the mirror stage as fragmentation, but as the birthing of her human identity. Moreover, Wolf-Alice does not have human language, nor can she understand wolf language, thus she creates subjectivity without the isolation that can occur when one has language. Wolf-Alice's identity is liminal; however, she is more authentic than an identity that contains solely bestial or solely human qualities. In Angela Carter's *Wolf-Alice,* Wolf-Alice's experience with coming of age and her interactions with the mirror allow her to transform her identity from animal objectivity to human subjectivity. Furthermore, her lack of human language grants Wolf-Alice the ability to remain in a liminal space that fosters an authentic self, combining both beastliness and humanity.

    Prior to Wolf-Alice's sexual maturation or discovery of the mirror, she lived in the state of animal objectivity without any human characteristics. Carter opens up the story with Wolf-Alice in her most raw form, stating that "she always runs on all fours," which instantly grounds the girl out of human reality (154). Wolves raised the girl, thus she behaves like them, relying on her keen sense of smell, sleeping in caves, and howling. Moreover, the narrator demonstrates that Wolf-Alice is unaware of her true self, claiming that "Nothing about her is human except that she is not a wolf," which highlights the fact that this girl lives in the most natural state of being (155). She does not have the social constructions of humanity surrounding her; therefore, she is subjected only to immediacy and "inhabits only the present tense" (155). Unlike humans, she does not have the concept of time or the concept of memories. Moreover, she does not have human language, but she can communicate with the wolves being unable to understand what the wolves say to her. She "grew amongst things she could neither name nor perceive" (158). Her lack of language prevents her from creating symbols for objects and hinders her from assimilating into any society (wolf or human), thus her "identity" stays in a liminal space. The implications of existing in complete objectivity for Wolf-Alice is that she is not fully accepted by the wolves, nor is she fully accepted by the humans, as she learns when the nuns abandon her in the Duke's mansion. However, abandoning her into the mansion of a being that is neither man nor beast will give the basis for Wolf-Alice's development as an authentic self, possessing human and animal qualities.

Wolf-Alice lives in a liminal space, as she is not wolf (the wolves do not accept her because she is an imperfect wolf), nor do the humans accept her, as the narrator points out.

Although Wolf-Alice exists in objectivity for a great part of her existence, her transformation into gaining humanity is marked by her sexual maturation. Prior to the start of Wolf-Alice's menarche, she does not understand the concept of time and is unaware of feelings such as shame. Upon her first menses, Wolf-Alice is shocked, and she seeks to clean up the mess, assuming that it is a wound caused by another wolf. The narrator claims, "so time passed, although she scarcely knew it. Then she began to bleed," which confirms that she was unaware of time prior to this experience (158). As her periods continue to show up, she "learned to expect those bleedings… [and]understood the circumambulatory principle of the clock perfectly" (160). Her awareness of time is directly related to her sexual awakening as a young female. In this sense, her menstruation makes her feel separate from her surroundings, and she begins to feel independent from her setting. Scott Dimovitz argues further that the "manifestation of her extrapolation of her subjectivity from biological processes" is critical to Wolf-Alice's development into a woman that contains both human and animal traits (15). Moreover, Wolf-Alice further develops human subjectivity in response to her menses as she begins to feel shame toward the mess that it makes. Wolf-Alice cleans up her bleedings, not because of "fastidiousness, but shame" (159). This shame is not commonplace for beasts, rather it is a characteristic reserved for humans that do something wrong in the presence of others. Here, Wolf-Alice sees her blood as unclean and learns to prepare for the bleedings as to hide the menstruations. Her human sexuality "brings her…into humanity" (Shanoes, 30). Wolf-Alice's coming-of-age experience is a marker for her transformation from the objective to the subjective. Additionally, Wolf-Alice's natural step into womanhood without societal constructs allows for her natural self to marry her wild traits alongside her budding humanity.

Wolf-Alice's menstruations are the beginning of the development of her identity, but her interactions with the mirror allow her to fully realize her transformation into a woman. Upon her first encounter with the mirror, she believes that the reflection is a cub-mate and attempts to play with it. Much like the mirror stage, she shows the signs of an infant within objectivity prior to understanding the image as self (full subjectivity). Throughout her sexual maturation the mirror acts as an "immovable surface between herself and she" with which she shares her female development (160). It is her sexual maturation and desire to share with her littermate that allows the mirror to become the tool that transforms her from the objective beast into the subjective woman. Wolf-Alice realizes that "her companion was ... a particularly ingenious variety of the shadow she cast" when she tries on the wedding dress (162). Her recognition of her shadow allows her to attain her self-image. She crosses over from the objective infant and into the subjective woman, as mentioned in Lacan's mirror stage, but because she sees it as a shadow of herself and not a misrecognition, she falls out of Lacanian mirror stage, thus allowing her to maintain female subjectivity external to the formative disciplines often imposed upon people during development (Lau, 91). Arguably, the mirror does not fragment Wolf-Alice; rather, she merges both the body and the ego into a liminal identity that is both empowered woman and innocent beast. Additionally, Wolf-Alice's "relation with the mirror was now far more intimate since she knew she saw herself within it" (162). The transformation of her identity is "marked by her budding sexuality ... she comes to recognize the reflection in the mirror" (Lau, 90). She gains an authentic self without the influences of wolf or human society, thus allowing her to combine harmoniously her natural state with her empowered state as a woman. Lastly, Wolf-Alice's reaction to trying on the dress further demonstrates her transformation into a mature woman. She examines her beauty in the mirror and is forced to walk on two feet due to the humanistic qualities of the dress. Dimovitz argues, "Wolf-Alice puts on the wedding dress and watches the transformation in the mirror" (13). After her transformation into a woman, she runs outside, "singing to the wolves ... because she knew how to wear clothes and so had put on the visible sign of her difference from [the wolves]" (162). She realizes that she is not a wolf "when she understands the nature of mirrors...and what is hidden behind them" (Shanoes, 31). Furthermore, Wolf-Alice ignores the minor restrictions of the dress as she tries to run in it, which demonstrates that her humanity is meshing with her beastliness; she accepts that she must learn to walk like a human if she wants to wear clothing. It is the dress, combined with her sexual maturation and understanding that she is not a wolf, that propels her into subjectivity.

Although it seems that Wolf-Alice's entrance into subjectivity would lead to her allowing social constructs to rid her of her animal nature, it is her lack of language that permits her to develop an authentic identity that preserves her animal instincts within her womanhood. Prior to Wolf-Alice, the narrator informs the reader that Wolf-Alice lives in a liminal state between wolf and human because "she does not understand [wolf] language even if she knows how to use it," and "she would have called herself a wolf, but she cannot speak" (154–155). Wolf-Alice cannot communicate with humans while being able to howl, however she cannot understand wolf howls. Lau states that this is positive to acquiring a balanced identity, as "Wolf-Alice is safely ensconced in the extralinguistic world" (Lau, 90). She has no language, which allows her to move through experiences using her senses rather than the social constructs of images. When the nuns attempt to teach her language, "[she] reverted ... to her natural state" (156). This "resistance to language" is due in part to her notion that she lives in the present and does not understand the social conventions that the nuns attempt to teach her (Lau, 90). Wolf-Alice is comfortable with her sensory abilities to communicate and understand the world; the language that the nuns try to teach her is resisted because she believes that she is a wolf. This resistance is what will allow her to develop into her womanhood without permanently rejecting her animal instincts. Even as Wolf-Alice matures, she keeps her wolf howls and does not interact with human language. Wolf-Alice is revered as "the wise child who leads them all and her silence and her howling a language as any language of nature" (158). This raw language married with her female identity is a "restatement of the motifs in a new Lacanian vocabulary" (Dimovitz, 13). The howling is the same as human language, however it does not attach words to images; rather, the howling only conveys senses and emotions. The lack of language eliminates her knowledge of appropriate human behavior and perspective on animalistic behavior. She remains authentic and innocent, yet she is empowered by her sexuality. Moreover, her lack of human language prevents her from being aware of what the Duke truly is, leading her to save him and ultimately bring him into being, as well. Wolf-Alice grants the werewolf-Duke agency by leaping on his bed to lick his wounds "without hesitation, without disgust," thus bringing the Duke "into being by her soft, moist, gentle tongue, finally, the face of the Duke" (164). She is the combination and the "insistence on the confluence of the human and the animal, the beautiful and the beastly" (Shanoes, 42). Although she has become a woman, she has not abandoned her animal instincts to take care of her master who is trapped in the liminal state. Her identity is fully formed in the instance that she heals the Duke with the language of her tongue. She does not need human language or wolf language to form an identity; in fact, her lack of language grants her an authentic identity that is in the liminal space between beastly and humane.

Forming an identity in a liminal space does not seem positive, however Wolf-Alice proves that a person can exist in the liminal space and create an identity that is true to the animal and the human self. Wolf-Alice grows from animal objectivity to human subjectivity within a liminal space. Her confrontation with her menstruation and her sexual maturation permit her to learn the concept of time and abandon her animalistic position in the ever-same present. This motion forward leads her to the Duke's mirror in which she learns that her reflection is her self-image as it grows from girl to woman. These events lead her to the realization that she is not a wolf, but a woman empowered by the raw sexuality of an animal. Moreover, she is able to marry her animal identity with her human identity due to her aversion to human language and inability to fully communicate with the wolves. She is unable to use symbols or understand human representations of life, thus allowing her to have the most authentic identity possible. While her innocence allows her to bring the Duke into being, as his reflection reappears in the mirror, this leads to the question: Will their combined humanities render them victims of social constructs or will they remain together in the harmonious liminal space of his blood chamber?

Pride and Prejudice: Propriety and Moderation

British novels written during the eighteenth and nineteenth century often wrestle with the rules of society and the expected behavior of men and women in the public arena. Frances Burney's novel *Evelina* introduces the importance of manners, politeness, and the function of social settings to serve as a location to find a suitable mate. The genre flourished and functioned as a guide for women with respect to the rules of behavior and the importance of social status. This guide created limitations on the acceptability of men and women interacting with one another outside of the same social class, while forcing a style of behavior that is appropriate in the public sphere. If Burney's novel sought to establish an artificial society that engaged within specific parameters, then Jane Austen's novel *Pride and Prejudice* sought to dismantle the artificiality in favor of genuine relationships regardless of social status. Moreover,

Austen exposed the frivolity of over-exposure within society and the arrogance of a complete disregard of society. Society in this instance does not refer to the governing body, rather the company of people that gather at a ball or assembly. The overarching plot of the novel argues for moderation of behavioral style that balances the personal and private sphere and allows one to maintain propriety while engaging in sociable activities that disregard social stations. In Jane Austen's *Pride and Prejudice*, the use of characterization, satire, and diction argue to preserve one's propriety while engaging with others in the social arena. Moreover, in establishing the moderation of social behavior that is neither over-the-top or underwhelmed, the novel attempts to dismantle the haughty societal rules that limit the interactions between people of differing stations.

The internal satire and characterization within *Pride and Prejudice* argue for individual preservation and the erasure of social delineation, but Austen's use of the words "society" and "propriety" within the novel are key to understanding the underlying motion to forgo social status while preserving one's reputation during the engagement with others. The word "society" throughout the novel does not stand for the institution; rather it stands for the company of people. For example, the quieter sister Mary admits that "society has claim on us all," and it is enjoyable to have "intervals of recreation and amusement" (Austen, 88). Furthermore, Elizabeth believes that every woman needs a "share of society" for recreation (Austen, 166). In both instances, the word is not being used as the law-governing body of people, but as a unit of people who enjoy company. In fact, "society" becomes synonymous with the word "company" in the novel. Society becomes a place for "practicing sociability" with people from the area without concern of social status (Sherry, 621). However, moderation of one's behavior while engaging with society becomes of utmost importance. Moreover, the word propriety takes on an important meaning to the characters of *Pride and Prejudice*, in that it stands for one's private life as much as it stands for one's reputation. For example, Mr.

Darcy did not want to socialize with Elizabeth because of her family's lack of propriety. This lack of propriety is the inability to balance one's style of behavior in the public and private spheres. Many of the Bennet women over-expose themselves in society, such as Lydia who elopes and Mrs. Bennet who is set on marrying off her daughters only to wealthy suitors. Later in the novel, Elizabeth realizes the "improprieties of Lydia's general behavior" and the impact it has on the family's "respectability in the world" (230–232). Thus, propriety no longer stands for high status and tradition, but rather it represents a style of behavior "which is ... careful not to violate the privacy ... of every individual" (Sherry, 618). Propriety becomes a central theme in the novel that must develop a definition that allows sociability and tradition to respect the individual and the individual's engagement with company. Darcy's definition of propriety must allow for social engagement, while Elizabeth must learn that propriety is about upholding one's individuality without losing respect within society.

Characterization is used to illustrate behavior at various levels within society that shows the need for a balance between social and private life that preserves propriety while gaily engaging with others. Characters such as Mr. Darcy, Lydia, and Mr. Bingley exemplify distinct levels of engagement within society with Lydia being overwhelming, Mr. Darcy uninvolved, and Mr. Bingley situated in the center. As Elizabeth notes, "Lydia's general behavior" shows a lack of respect for her own propriety and the Bennet family's propriety as she gallantly exposes her private life to the public (Austen, 230). She flirts with men and ultimately elopes with a man she barely knows; her overexposure in the social world damages her reputation and creates a further rift between the station of the Bennets and the station of other families such as the Bingleys. In James Sherry's article "*Pride and Prejudice*: The Limits of Society," he points out that "there are limits to society and sociability," which Lydia does not respect (612). The lack of propriety presents her as a silly woman not worth the attention of people above her station. Alternatively,

Mr. Darcy is reserved and arrogant in the company of the people from Netherfield, as they do not meet his standards, or perhaps, his aim for propriety is much higher than he recognizes. The women feel that "his manners gave a disgust which turned the tide of his popularity," as he did not appropriately engage with society (Austen, 12). Moreover, he "declined being introduced to any other lady" outside of his close circle of company (Austen, 13). Darcy refuses to take part with the assembly, as he believes there is no woman there that stands at his level. Darcy is "antisocial" and his "discretion [is] protective of the individual" to a point that he excludes himself from social activities (Sherry, 612–613). His behavior is traditional in the attempt to preserve his social status, although he must change his method of engagement to discover that social status is not the factor here, but propriety. Lastly, Mr. Bingley is the perfect example of a person engaging in society and maintaining a balance of personal and private spheres. Bingley "had a pleasant countenance" and "danced every dance" regardless of his social status

(Austen, 12). He gaily engages at the social events and keeps his propriety by avoiding conversations that discuss intimate affairs. Bingley provides an example for Lydia and Mr. Darcy on the "responsibility" to be engaged with society, while keeping "distance" that preserves one's propriety without disengaging from enjoying company (Sherry, 612). The characters' choice to characterize persons on all parts of the spectrum and letting the ones at the extreme side suffer guides the reader into valuing moderation of one's personal and private life, while actively engaging in company. Bingley's choice to ignore his social status and enjoy the activities leads him to meet Jane with ease, but with Darcy it takes nearly two hundred pages before he can be with Elizabeth by readjusting his attitude on social interactions.

    The characterization argues for moderation in society, while Austen's use of satire helps dismantle the tradition of social status and the attitude that goes toward those that attempt to cross its line. Elizabeth's snarky wit satirizes much of the arrogant social class tradition throughout the novel.

Elizabeth is gregarious and engages with society members regardless of their rank. For example, after discovering that Mr. Darcy was listening to her conversations she says, "Did you not think, Mr. Darcy, that I expressed myself uncommonly well just now" to point out that her rank has nothing to do with her refined propriety or intelligence (Austen, 25). Her focus is brilliant as she attempts to render his social status useful with her wit to show that he has "too great a dependence upon," the artificial aspects of rank and status (Sherry, 614–15). Elizabeth further satirizes upper class people through her interactions with Lady Catherine. Upon the first interaction with Lady Catherine, who definitely demonstrates her rank, Elizabeth dismantles tradition by disagreeing with Lady Catherine about her sisters enjoying "their share of society and amusement," although the eldest sisters are not yet married (Austen, 165). Elizabeth further removes Lady Catherine from her artificial station in Chapter 56 during the discussion of the Darcy engagement rumor. After Lady Catherine travels so far to discover the truth and then insults Elizabeth, Elizabeth answers, "I wonder you took the trouble of coming so far" for news that the could scarcely believe to be true (Austen, 343). Elizabeth pokes fun at the worry of Lady Catherine's regard for social station. It is clear that she is worried that Mr. Darcy would marry somebody she considers so low in society, yet she personally shows up at Elizabeth's home for answers. Austen satirizes social status through these interactions and successfully disengages the artificial lines as her satire "is subversive of society" and brings Lady Catherine to Elizabeth's level (Sherry, 614). More so, one could argue that she elevates Elizabeth above Lady Catherine and Mr. Darcy since she does not see the same lines that separate one class from another. It is a "devaluation of sociability" in the sense that the tradition of keeping within the boundaries of societal rules is broken to free the individual from societal restrictions (Sherry, 617). Elizabeth's satirical wit toward social status will later free Mr. Darcy from his own design and allow for the social lines to be blurred in the consummation of their love.

The decision to engage in society in a way that integrates men and women from all social classes opens up the opportunity for genuine relationships to form. Mr. Darcy needed to remove himself from his disregard of company he was not well acquainted with, while other characters needed to learn proper behavior within the public sphere. The use of characterization seeks to find a balance of private and social life that does not encroach upon individuality, nor crush the purpose of social engagements. Austen uses opposites to highlight the extremes of social behavior, while placing Mr. Bingley in the middle to demonstrate that a person of high social status can happily engage with those outside of a wealthy circle. Moreover, the novel seeks to erase the lines of social status by placing all characters in the same room and forcing them to find the proper balance between the private and public spheres. Austen's use of satire and diction through Elizabeth's intelligent language further pulls apart traditions and the artificiality of social status. Love does surpass pride, prejudice, and the unnecessary walls that attempt to separate those that are meant to be together. Furthermore, the work establishes propriety as a protection of the individual within the social sphere of company. *Pride and Prejudice* serves as an extension to the novel of manners, developed in the eighteenth century in order to give freedom to individuals who choose to participate in social activities with person of all ranks, and ultimately individuality is able to surpass the stuffy rules of old tradition.

Their Eyes Were Watching God: Intersectionality of the Mule and Janie's Hair and How Janie's Claims Her Identity

During Reconstruction women struggled to claim their identity as black and female as the taste of slavery washed out of America's mouth. In many ways women were treated as less than human and less than other animals, as they fell below all other Americans (if we reference white men, black men, white women, and then black women) in society. They were expected to obey their husbands and sit silent behind the ongoing of society. It left them with little space to discover and embrace their identity as an African American woman. The oppression that these women were subjected to is known as "intersectionality," a term coined by feminist Kimberle Crenshaw. Intersectionality examines how the intersecting constructs of gender and race oppress a person. Together these oppressive forces can hinder a person from embracing their identity. The forces of intersectionality with regards to gender and race is witnessed in Zora Neal Hurston's *Their Eyes Were Watching God*, a narrative plot that follows Janie Starks through three marriages to men who oppress her and a society that does not accept African Americans as fully human. Hurston uses the mule and Janie's hair as the symbols to express the racial and gender oppression exerted on Janie who represents all African American women during the Reconstruction period. Moreover, both symbols progressively change from repressed symbols to liberated symbols as Janie surpasses the effects of intersectionality. Literary critics Keiko Dilbeck, Ryan Simmons, Missy Dehn Kubitschek, Isis H. Simmons, and Ann Garry evaluate Hurston's depiction of Janie as the representation of the African American woman experiencing intersectionality and her ability to rise above it and claim her identity, by which I will expand upon and examine how the symbols of the mule and the hair deviant from race to gender and from oppressed to free. In *Their Eyes Were Watching God*, the protagonist Janie Starks overcomes the intersectionality of racial and gender oppression, which Hurston symbolizes through a mule and Janie's hair; there is a transformation from oppressed to freedom that Janie grabs ahold of and claims her identity in the face of an oppressive society.

  Janie experiences racial oppression as a woman who identifies herself as an African American. Hurston symbolizes this oppression of Janie and of all African Americans through the mule that surfaces twice within the narrative. Hurston references the black community as "uh pullin' and uh haulin' and uh sweatin' and uh doin'" for the "bossman" from the time the sun breaks the horizon to the moment that they close their eyes to sleep (Hurston, 22). It demonstrates that even with the elimination of slavery racism still exists. One could argue that metaphorically Janie is the mule of Eatonville. She is oppressed as a black person who is treated as less than human, much like the mule that is worked until it is broken and eventually led out to die. For example, they say, "you think youse white folks by de way you act" in reference to her outspoken and outwardly different identity with a community that expects her to behave a certain way (29). She is chastised for having proud mannerisms because black people, especially black women, are supposed to be submissive to authority.

The fact that Janie must deal with her black identity as being something that holds her back is associated with the negative impacts of intersectionality. According to Isis Settles' *Use of an Intersectional Framework to Understand Black Women's Racial and Gender Identities*, a black woman "strongly identifies with [her] race" more than with her gender, which can lead to "negative psychological outcomes" (590). The pressures of identifying as a woman and as black are what hinder Janie from embracing her identity whilst she is married to Jody Starks. Jody oppresses Janie's association with African American culture by restraining her from sitting on the porches and telling stories about the mule, which parallels the mistreatment of the mule of Eatonville who is "Jus' evil and don't want to be led" (Hurston, 52). Both Janie and the mule are made to seem lesser due to their identities. Moreover, Kubitschek in "'Tuh De Horizon and Back': The Female Quest in *Their Eyes Were Watching God*" claims "Janie's reaction to the cruel pursuit of the mule is in one sense a reaction to her own plight" as a black person struggling to hold onto her racial identity under the pressures of an unaccepting society (112). While I agree that the mule symbolizes the racial oppression of Janie, I would expand upon that argument to say that the mule fuses together the oppression of racial and gender identities.

    The mule compares to the oppression of African Americans, but it intersects with Janie's identity as a woman, too. In Keiko Dilbeck's *Symbolic Representation of Identity In Hurston's* Their Eyes Were Watching God, Janie's empathy for the mule "is often seen as Janie's own sense of entrapment" as a female being pushed down by her abusive relationships (103). Janie empathizes with the mule because the men of Eatonville are treating it inhumanely. She is satisfied when Jody saves the mule from the abuse, but he bans her from celebrating the mule's life when it dies as a way to force her "into submission" (Hurston, 67). Moreover, Hurston compares women to mules through Janie's Nanny stating, "De nigger woman is de mule of de world" and is responsible for carrying everybody's load without reward (14). Thus, Janie is a mule suffering from oppression as a woman. In *The Hierarchy Itself: Hurston's Their Eyes Were Watching God and the Sacrifice of Narrative Authority*, Simmons points out that "Joe's authority ... replicates the authority by which whites have oppressed African Americans," and he "uses the oppression of Janie as both an African American and a woman" (185).

As the mule symbolizes the racial oppression of Janie's black identity, it morphs into the symbol that enables her release from the racial oppression. Jody saving the mule from further abuse prompts Janie to contemplate her own path to a liberated identity as a black woman. She responds to Jody's action with rhetoric stating "Freein dat mule makes uh mighty big man" as a statement that paradoxes his oppression of Janie (Hurston, 55). The introduction of the mule into Janie's world allows her "to conceptualize a true quest for her identity [because] she sees herself and all former slaves in that mule" (Kubitschek, 110). The mule is the start of Janie's independence and it "initiates that downfall of Jody" who has been her oppressor since they were married (Simmons, 185). The mule gives Janie the opportunity to free herself from one of the oppressions pushing her into a subhuman status. Ann Garry, a feminist expert in intersectionality argues that the oppressions can break apart from one another as a person no longer allows it to affect their identity, which is what happens with the death of Jody and of the mule; Janie is released from her racial oppression (839–840). Janie frees her identity from feeling negatively about her black heritage and embraces that identity; however, Janie must still unravel herself from the oppression that she faces as a black woman.

    Janie's identity breaks free from racial oppression, but she must work harder to escape the oppression she faces on her gender identity. Janie is raised by her Nanny, an old woman who teaches Janie that she needs a husband (and to obey him dutifully) to survive the world. Unfortunately, this mantra haunts Janie through two abusive relationships that force her to suppress her identity. Hurston uses Janie's hair to symbolize female empowerment, as well as the impacts of gender oppression. Throughout the novel, men actively notice Janie's "great rope of black hair, which signifies her as a strong female going against societal expectations and avoiding oppression (Hurston, 2). Janie did not always wear her hair down, as her first two husbands castrate her female empowerment by forcing her to tie up her hair. First, Logan Killicks admires her hair, but after seeing its power he "made [Janie] let down [her] hair for de last time," which starts the gender oppression that Janie experiences for much of the novel (Hurston, 16). Thereafter, she meets and marries Jody Starks who praises her for being a beautiful woman, but quickly the marriage turns into a dominator-oppressed relationship in which Starks does everything in his power to put Janie into a powerless role. He does so successfully. Starks oppresses Janie's womanhood by physically abusing her, but more importantly by treating her as though she "ain't got no particular place" in the world other than as the role of the obedient wife (Hurston, 30). To strip her of her feminine power, "he ordered Janie to tie up her hair" under kerchiefs (52). By tying her hair up, she did not have power as a woman in the community. The townspeople noticed and wondered why Janie allowed Jody to "keep her head tied lak some ole 'oman" (47). Janie was aware that Jody was oppressing her as she felt "this business of the head-rag irked her," yet she kept her hair up to avoid conflict (51). As their marriage progresses, Janie's dissent for Jody's oppressive behavior accumulates with her (especially with the event of the mule). Janie begins to realize that "she belongs to no one but herself" (Dilbreck, 103). The event of Jody's death marks the start of Janie's liberation, and "she tore the kerchief and let down her plentiful hair" allowing her to regain her femininity (Hurston, 83). Nevertheless, she does not fully regain her identity in that moment as she "tied it back up again," illustrating how effective the intersection of racial and gender oppression has been on Janie's identity (Settles, 590). Quickly after Starks' death, she is able to let go of her oppressor by finally burning the kerchiefs (Hurston, 85). Letting down her hair down allows her to complete her quest in finding her identity and overcoming the weight of the intersecting inequalities placed on her gender and race. With the exits of both of her husbands, letting down her hair allows Janie to escape the restraints of both of her husbands (Simmons, 181). This freedom allows Janie to meet Tea Cake, the only man that accepts her for her powerful female presence and openly enjoys her beautiful black hair. Together they celebrate each other's identities, which teaches Janie that submission to another is not required to be an independent woman who wants to be loved by others.

  Hurston's *Their Eyes Were Watching God* is a powerful narrative demonstrating the harsh effects of racial and gender oppression, as well as the impact that they can have when they intersect within one's identity. Janie Starks faces severe racial oppression from the white and black communities that she grows up in because she never quite fits in with one or the other. As she matures, she identities with African Americans and we see her racial oppression symbolized by the image of the mule. The mule serves as a representation of African American oppression during slavery and thereafter, which Janie successfully overcomes through rhetoric and the demise of Jody, who symbolizes white oppression. Moreover, the mule symbolizes the African American woman, specifically as a person who is less human than all others. Furthermore, Hurston uses Janie's hair to symbolize female empowerment and how the implications of oppression on women can force them to hide their hair (gender identity). This novel demonstrates how an African American woman identifies with her race and gender, as well as the long journey it takes to accept one's identity in the face of oppression. This is Hurston's feminine manifesto to bring awareness to the African American community that racial and gender oppression is unacceptable. I question the features of intersectionality and how gender and racial oppression could eliminated with texts such as these. Could Janie really be the role model for all other minorities?

Fosdick: The Foil of *Ragged Dick* and the Highlighted Values of Industrial Capitalism

Industrial capitalism marked an increase in free enterprise and American men becoming members of a machine that fed men up the rungs and launched them into careers as successful businessmen. It marked the separation of the male-centric corporate realm and the female-centric domestic realm, also. In Horatio Alger's *Ragged Dick* the characters Dick and Fosdick exemplify what it means to be a member of industrial capitalism, as well as what defines those who are not allowed to take part in the business world. *Ragged Dick* follows the rising young man, Dick, as he climbs his way from a shoe-shining boy to a respectable, capitalist man. Young Dick shares part of his experience with Fosdick, a boy with domesticated characteristics. His person is perpendicular to that of Dick. Fosdick is the foil of Dick. Moreover, Alger uses allusion to demonstrate that the innate characteristics of Dick are those that are innate to the success of capitalism and those who are to be successful within capitalism. Recently, Alyssa Kuhlman wrote in *The Foil of Fosdick* that Fosdick served as a foil to Dick and that Dick requires three qualities to succeed as an industrial capitalist. Whilst many of her ideas are concurrent with my argument, there are several points that do not support Fosdick's purpose as a foil and the innate characteristic of an industrial capitalist. In Alger's *Ragged Dick*, he uses Fosdick as a foil to highlight the gendered properties of industrial capitalism, while using the personal traits of Dick to allude to the values of industrial capitalism and the qualities required in a man to become a successful member of the capitalist industry.

The properties of a successful capitalist are highlighted through the contrast of Dick and Fosdick using a marital-like relationship. Dick embodies the characteristics of professional masculinity, while Fosdick embodies the characteristics of domesticity. For example, the relationship between Dick and Fosdick is similar to that of a marriage: the two boys sleep in the same bed, Dick provides for Fosdick, and

Fosdick is less manly than Dick. Particularly, possessing an education is a significant property that divides Dick and Fosdick into a relationship with a masculine and feminine counterpoint. In Kuhlman's argument, she infers that an education is a quality needed by a successful capitalist, thus making for a stronger capitalist (thereby more masculine). She states, "Dick's uneducated background holds him back," however I disagree because Fosdick held an education, yet he was still an unsuccessful bootblack (Kuhlman, 3). It is true that education is important to becoming successful; however, it does not prop up Fosdick, as he continues to receive less pay than Dick, plus Alger infers through the text that an education is not a manly quality. Alger states that Fosdick "had devoted too much time to study, for he was not naturally robust," inferring that those who are educated with a liking to reading are less suited for the hard-working industry of capitalism (Alger, 89). This reference implies that Fosdick's slender physique is not an innate quality of an industrial capitalist, while Dick's experience in the business world and his manly figure are things that lift a man into the success of industrial capitalism. It further implies that there is a clear line between the business and domestic sectors of one's life. Moreover, Alger illustrates that less masculinity in industrial capitalism equates to less success. For example, "Dick had more of a business turn than Henry ... so that his earnings were greater" (Alger, 93). Thus, even though both boys were in the same business, Dick regularly made more wages than Fosdick, which provides insight into the wheelworks of industrial capitalism. The capitalist world is not for those with feminine interests, i.e. reading and education, instead the masculine, ambitious man is built for success in professional/business industry.

    More importantly, Alger uses Dick's personal traits to allude to what a capitalist should possess in order to become successful in the business world. Alger's "rags to riches" metaphor in this story is an allusion to how industrial capitalism functions to pull a young man up through the rungs and into a successful position in business. Dick starts out poor, yet he has the qualities needed to be a successful capitalist. Kuhlman's argument stated that a successful capitalist must possess honesty, a strong work ethic, and an education (Kuhlman, 1). I agree that Dick needs to possess these qualities to a certain extent, but I do not agree that without one of these qualities he would not be successful in his business ventures. The most important traits were those that were innate to Dick, rather than the properties that had to be ascertained from an external source such as an education. According to Alger, a man needed to be honest, ambitious, possess luck, and be nurtured by another successful capitalist in order to become a successful businessperson. Honesty and ambition are Dick's innate traits for success, while luck and a helping hand are aids that can propel Dick faster into success, yet they are not mandatory for such success. Dick's honesty was his most important quality to make him successful in industrial capitalism. Dick was "so far good that he could appreciate the goodness of others," and "His nature was a noble one, and had saved him from all mean faults" (Alger, 8 and 92). This implies that

Dick's innate honesty is required in capitalism. Moreover, Kuhlman points out that Dick's innate honesty was present in his physical description, as Alger points to his "honest face," which dictates that he has a trustworthiness that is desired in the business world (Kuhlman, 1). These points allude that all industrial capitalists must be honest and noble in his business dealings in order to be successful. It is important to parallel this point of Dick's honesty with a point that was made in Kuhlman's argument: Kuhlman claimed that Dick was innately honest, but then countered this point, stating that Dick was deceptive due to his lack of education (Kuhlman, 3). This is paradoxical and does not exemplify the nature of young Dick. In fact, the education that Dick achieved did not change his innate qualities; however, it did make him a more presentable businessperson. Throughout Alger's portrayal, Dick was not deceptive by any means. In fact, Alger states that Dick "would not steal, or cheat, or impose" since "his nature was a noble one" (Alger, 7). Dick was an honest young man and gaining an education gave him an edge, however, it was not the determining factor in Dick's success. Furthermore, one's ambitious nature is a required trait, as Alger writes, "Now, in the boot blacking business, as well as in higher avocations, the same rule prevails, that energy and industry are rewarded, and indolence suffers" (Alger, 10). Likewise, Kuhlman states, "[Dick's] smart initiative" is what "drives him" to be a successful capitalist (Kuhlman, 3). Where Kuhlman and I disagree, this is a point in which we parallel our arguments, as we both concur that Dick's natural ambition is a stronger driving force than external forces such as an education or luck. Dick pushed himself as a young bootblack earning a respectable amount of money, and, upon his realization that he could be a respectable businessman, he made the necessary steps to remove himself from poverty and aim for a higher standard of living.

Additionally, success in capitalism comes with the help of luck and a helping hand, too. Dick says, "'I went to a fortun' teller once and she told me I was born under a lucky star . . . and I should have a rich man for my particular friend, who would make my fortun'" (Alger, 126). In every case, Dick's success is attributed to his innate qualities and the steps that he takes to become a respectable man. He uses his natural qualities to attract outside help. His honesty and ambition project him into the attention of the professional men such as Mr. Whitney, who helps him by putting him on the path to being a successful capitalist. Kuhlman states, "one with a stronger appearance of honesty . . . receives a helping hand from a benefactor" (Kuhlman, 2). Her argument is correct in claiming that one's innate honesty, the same honesty that was present on Dick's face, is what aids in gaining a helping hand into capitalism. Not only is Mr. Whitney the helping hand that allows Dick to succeed in industrial capitalism, but it is Dick's run into luck as well. He was lucky enough to overhear the conversation between Mr. Whitney and Frank, which was one of the major stepping-stones for Dick into the life of a successful capitalist. Another way to look at Dick's character traits and those that help him is to view it as an allusion to what it means to be a part of industrial capitalism. One must carve out his own success, however, it is expected that an older man must mold a young man in order to get into the business as well. Alger leans toward the idea that industrial capitalism is an honest, ambitious workforce that requires hard work and dedication, rather than relying on one's reputation to be successful in the industry.

    Industrial capitalism revolutionized American culture. *Ragged Dick* addresses the gendering of the society and the values of industrial capitalism. Fosdick, acting as a foil to Dick, highlights the requirement for masculinity in the business world and further shows the divide between what genders are and are not supposed to be as a part of the capitalist sector. Moreover, Alger details the innate character traits that are the values of industrial capitalism and the steps one must take to be successful. Kuhlman presents the ideologies of industrial capitalism to be rigid and mandatory; however, I am left to believe that Alger was pointing to a more indirect purpose of using Fosdick as a foil of Dick's innate qualities. Alger indirectly points out that these ideologies are masks of what industrial capitalism truly entails. Was industrial capitalism truly about honesty and ambition? Alternatively, was it about making the most profit possible without fretting over the implications on society? Dick is an honest and ambitious boy, but he does not become a respectable young man until he dons clean clothes and is taken under the wing of an already successful businessman. Is this the same mask that industrial capitalism portrayed? Capitalism may look wonderful in a clean suit, but underneath that suit may not be the inherently noble qualities that young *Ragged Dick* holds onto. Moreover, Alger's portrayal of Dick and Fosdick's relationship suggests that masculinity belongs in business, while femininity belongs in the domestic sector of society. *Ragged Dick* is a prime example of the double standards that have plagued men and women for centuries. *Ragged Dick* successfully uses a foil and allusion to demonstrate the values of Industrial Capitalism and how it worked during the era in which the work was written.

A New England Nun: Unconventional Sexuality and Autonomy

Sexuality and independence were not features of a woman's life in the latter half of the nineteenth century; however, several female authors penning local color (American Regionalism) subtly inserted notions of women actively choosing solitary lifestyles, embracing alternative sexuality (whether this be self-love or homosexuality), and refuting the societal expectations of women through allusion, character, and symbolism. In Mary W. Freeman's "A New England Nun," Freeman uses the spinster-like characteristics of Louisa Willis to demonstrate how a woman takes control of her sexuality and identity by refuting the social expectations of women during the late nineteenth century. A close reading of Louisa's interactions with her home, Joe Dagget, and her chained dog reveal that she is preserving her homosexuality from a critical society, as well as securing her identity from male interference. Many critics including Hirsch and Pryse have elaborated heavily on Freeman's protagonist as a woman of a compulsive nature and a woman who is sexually repressed, however, there are many critics reading this story with an eye in the way of queer modernism and feminism. Through this lens, Louisa's lesbianism comes to the surface. Recently, Ben Couch in "The No-Man's Land of 'A New England Nun'" argues that Louisa's sexuality was embodied in Caesar, the dog, and that the story is driven by her need to protect her self-love and identity from society. Couch touches on the personification of Caesar as a connection between Joe and Louisa, as well as the idea that Louisa feared her wild sexuality. Whilst I agree with Couch in some aspect, I believe that Louisa was not afraid of her sexuality—she had no choice but to remain alone with her homosexuality due to the climate of the time. In "A New England Nun," Louisa is a lesbian who chooses to preserve her sexuality and identity from society by remaining a "spinster"; Freeman demonstrates Louisa's control of her sexuality and identity through symbolism and allusion between Louisa, her domesticity, her dog, and her empty engagement to Joe Dagget.

Freeman's decision to make both domesticity and order Louisa's top priorities highlights an understated distaste for men and for men to be a part of her identity. Rather than avoid domesticity because of its negative connotations, Louisa embraces its feminine nature and allows her need for order in the home to empower her to take hold of her identity; her home becomes a safe house of her autonomy and she is not willing to relinquish it for a man or society. Louisa's need for order symbolizes her desire to control her identity. For example, when Joe Dagget rearranges the books, she "kept eyeing them with mild uneasiness" and "rose and changed the position of the books" (Freeman, 715). She actively exerts her will on her identity in front of Joe Dagget to show that she will not change herself for him. Had she been worried about the implications of a woman correcting a man's actions, she would have waited until he left her home. Ben Couch mentions that Hirsch calls this behavior "obsessive neurosis," which both Couch and I disagree with (Couch, 2). This is not a compulsive behavior; her need to clean up after Joe Dagget's intrusion on her home is a signpost of her desire to keep her identity and her sexuality to herself. It is "a desperate struggle to retain the essential Louisa" (Couch, 3). Louisa's personality is neat and orderly, and, with an impending marriage to a man that she does not love in the future, she is fighting for what defines who she is.

On the other hand, I do not agree with Couch's argument that she is "[preserving] her sexual fantasy" through her orderliness or detraction from Joe Dagget, but her need for order and femininity alludes to the notion that she is a lesbian who wants to keep the masculine society away from something that is integral to her identity (Couch, 10). Freeman points out in several sections of the story that men are not welcome in Louisa's life and she prefers a womanly environment. For example, Louisa cannot "remember that ever in her life she had mislaid one of these little feminine appurtenances," because her life was surrounded by "maidenly possessions"

(Freeman, 715). Louisa keeps her feminine domesticity in order as much as she reigns in her sexuality and identity. Furthermore, Louisa views Joe Dagget's presence negatively, noting that "He seemed to fill up the whole room" when he visited her so much so that when he left "Louisa got a dust pan and brush, and swept Joe Dagget's track carefully" to guarantee that after he was gone there was no male presence remaining in her home—in herself (Freeman, 716–717). Louisa does everything to remove the male presence from her home because Joe is a threat to Louisa's sexuality and identity (7). If Freeman does not successfully demonstrate Louisa's sexuality in that passage, she allows it to shine when Louisa is thinking about what marrying Joe Dagget will do to her sexuality:

> she had visions, so startling that she half repudiated them as indelicate, of course masculine belongings strewn about in endless litter; of dust and disorder arising necessarily from a coarse masculine presence in the midst of all this delicate harmony (719).

Louisa fears the inclusion of Joe Dagget in her life because it will destroy her sexuality and her ability to control it once it enters a world of disorder and masculinity. Couch claims that this is Louisa's realization that her "self-love" will be ruined "within the bounds of marriage," but I do not wholly agree that it is self-love unless we define self-love as her independence (Couch, 4). Couch defines Louisa's self-love as masturbation, but the allusion in the story points to her homosexuality and desire to live an autonomous life (Couch, 10). There is no place for masculinity in Louisa's life, and she will go to many lengths to preserve her identity and sexuality from expectations put upon her as a woman in this time.

Another allusion to Louisa's homosexuality and desire to control it is her decision to remain in an empty engagement with Joe Dagget. For fourteen years Louisa lives alone, engaged to a man who left her to work in Australia. What woman in the nineteenth century did that? Couch claims that it is her noble character that helps her keep the engagement, but I disagree and would argue that Louisa uses the engagement as an illusion to preserve her solitude and her sexuality. Louisa reveals that Joe's absence was the "greatest happening of all" since it put her on a path "so narrow that there was no room for anyone at her side" (Freeman, 718). She revels in her solitude. Moreover, Louisa recognizes that her sexuality prevents her from sharing her life with another, thus she "removes herself from society" (Couch, 6). We can infer that Dagget's physical absence stands for the fact that Louisa and Joe are sexually incompatible because of Louisa's sexual attraction to all things feminine.

Additionally, Louisa reveals that she never expected the engagement to end in marriage because she thought that he would never return, or if he did return he would not follow through with the engagement. Every small detail that Freeman reveals through allusion and Louisa's character demonstrates that she was never going to marry Dagget because that would mean burying her sexuality and her identity along with her love for femininity. Upon the ending of the engagement, Louisa is satisfied and relieved. Couch argues that Louisa is emotionally distressed from the breaking of the engagement, citing that Louisa felt "sexual rejection" from Joe, but Couch extracts a moment from an entire scene to make this argument without connecting it to the next emotion that Louisa experiences (Couch, 5). After Louisa discovers that Joe has feelings for Lily Dyer, she went home and "wept a little," but "she hardly knew why" until she woke up the next morning feeling "like a queen who, after fearing lest her domain be wrested away from her, sees it firmly ensued in her possession" (Freeman, 722). Louisa is free to be who she wants to be and is no longer concerned that Joe will take away her identity and her sexuality through a marriage that would have not given either of them sexual or personal satisfaction. Louisa did not cry because she was being rejected, she was crying out of relief for not having to abandon her homosexuality to fit into a society that was not willing to accept her identity. It is true that by ending the engagement Louisa must keep her sexuality restrained, but the choice between "[killing] her sexuality or keep[ing] it on a chain" was an easy decision for her to make. Here she is free to control her sexuality within her home and through the chains that tie down Caesar, symbolic of her wild sexuality that she compulsively restrains from pouncing on the world.

While Louisa's adherence to an empty engagement protects her sexuality from being buried, Freeman symbolizes Louisa's sexuality in her dog Caesar. Caesar has been chained to his dog house for fourteen years after he bit a neighbor and was forced to remain restrained or be put to death. Louisa adamantly restrains the dog, never letting him off of his leash. The chained Caesar symbolizes Louisa's chained sexuality as a lesbian. We are introduced to Caesar with "the clank of a chain, and a large yellow-and-white dog appeared at the door of his tiny hut, which was half hidden among the tall grasses and flowers" as Louisa goes to feed him corn cakes and biscuits (Freeman, 715). Perhaps the most interesting token of this scene is the wildly tall grass in comparison to her neat garden and meticulously kept home. If Caesar is to be Louisa's sexuality on a chain, then this tall grass is the "wild zone" in which she allows her sexuality to flourish, unlike anywhere else in her home or society. Thus, Louisa is not forgoing her sexuality, rather "she retains reign over it" and permits it "to live in this wild zone" since it cannot be allowed into the streets of society because society would be destroyed by it (Couch, 10–11). Louisa fears unchaining the dog, calling him "a very monster of ferocity" and picturing the dog going on a rampage in the village should he ever be released from his chains (Freeman, 720). It is interesting that she thinks of Caesar as such a monster since Freeman notes that "Caesar was a veritable hermit of a dog" (719). Caesar symbolizes what Louisa thinks of her own sexuality. Homosexuality was not socially acceptable during Louisa's life (and Freeman's life), thus she knows that she must keep the dog chained to the hut even if the dog appears to be a harmless animal who has paid his punishment. Unfortunately, Louisa is trapped like Caesar. Her identity and sexuality must be kept inside her home and on a chain in order to preserve it from the critical eyes of society. Some critics may look at this as Louisa repressing her sexuality, which in part she is forced to repress it from society, but I would argue that by staying single Louisa is fighting back against these societal expectations. Staying unmarried, she is allowed to let her sexuality grow around the hut even if it means that she must ostracize herself from living with society, yet when did Louisa ever seem like a character who wanted to fit into "the bounds of societal opinion" (Couch, 3)? Moreover, Couch mentions that Louisa fears her sexuality, stating that "Louisa is afraid of and enchanted by her own sexuality," but I disagree because it seems that she fears what society would do to her if they discovered her wild sexuality was let off of the chains.

Female sexuality has always been an underscored subject within society, thus it is not a surprise that the character of Louisa has been glossed as a spinster preserving her independence. "A New England Nun" is Freemans elegy to female sexuality, more importantly how societal constraints can hinder one's ability to live the sexuality that they identify with. Ben Couch opened up a new argument on Louisa, her sexuality, and her identity as a woman in the late nineteenth century. His development of Caesar as her sexuality and the relationship between Louisa and Joe provide a platform to read Louisa as a character that defied social norms. Through evaluation of the symbolism of Caesar, in combination with Louisa's reaction to Joe Dagget's disloyalty and her preference for a feminine environment, it was clear that Freeman intended for Louisa to be read as a lesbian trapped in a society over-developed by masculine characteristic and expectations. Louisa is unable to reveal her homosexuality, but she does everything that she can to preserve her autonomy and identity whilst also keeping her sexuality without sacrificing it for a loveless marriage. Louisa is a role model for women who want to carve out their own identity without feeling the pressures to behave like a woman, whatever that is supposed to entail. "A New England Nun" started a conversation on female sexuality and how we can get society to embrace and tolerate those that do not fit into the constraints of society. Freeman's short fiction leaves me asking society, "When will we be able to allow everybody into the social ring?"

The Female American: Marginalized Identity Transcends Patriarchy

Early American literature is full of texts that celebrate American colonization and exemplify the successful assimilation of an "American" identity into a European identity, but none demonstrates the power of a marginalized female biracial identity as Unca Eliza Winkfield's *The Female American*. Unca Eliza is marginalized and liminal due to her status as a biracial female living in a Euro-American atmosphere; she is thrust into Englishness although she is not fully Anglicized. This mixed-blood status grants her the authority as a female to stand on a plane equal to that of her male counterparts, as she pushes against patriarchal control. Unca Eliza, a biracial and bicultural female who travels between America and Europe, and gets abandoned on an island, is able to transcend the traditional patriarchal suffocation and develop agency without sacrificing her marginalized identities. Winkfield uses authorial power to portray a character that finds a space in which she can be both Indian and European without having to conform to either identity wholly. In Unca Eliza Winkfield's *The Female American*, the author uses concepts of feminism and otherness to allow Unca Eliza's liminal identity to transcend traditional gender roles and patriarchal colonization.

    Unca Eliza crosses traditional gender boundaries due to her ability to take part in masculine activities; her biracial and bicultural affiliation allows her to do so without much refutation. Throughout the novel, from Unca Eliza's childhood to her decision to remain on the island with her cousin, she performs in masculine manners, unlike typical European women. For example, Unca Eliza exudes a masculine dominance in her position as an Indian princess living amongst European men. She claims, "I might have been a queen . . . but I declined" as she wanted to reside with her father and to become educated (Winkfield, 49). Her decision forefronts her power over her agency and proves that as a bicultural woman, she is forging an American identity through her Indian mother and English father. According to Cathy Rex's argument in her book *Indianness and Womanhood: Textualizing the Female American Self*, "Indian women who were of 'mixed blood' as well as Anglicized, however, were even more potentially insurgent because of their capacity to rupture both the racist and gendered discourses" (224). Thus, Unca Eliza is free to create her own role as a woman who is neither Indian nor European. She is a threat to the patriarchal-created feminine role, as she steps out of the traditional role to carve out a feminine identity that is not oppressed by Englishmen.

Moreover, Unca Eliza steps out of the boundaries of the traditional European woman to engage in masculine activities. She can do so because she represents the masculine "Nativeness" from her mother's blood and the European civility of her father's heritage. The combination of the two allows her to cross back and forth between roles and cultures. Unca Eliza is allowed "the same learned education as [her uncle's] son" in hopes that she "might make one of their society" (Winkfield, 50). Unca is given the chance to be an educated member of society, which later becomes part of her reason for surviving on the uninhabited island. Her knowledge of religious scripture combined with her education in rhetoric allows her to adapt the Bible into a discourse that the Indians will understand (107). This allows her to take control of the Indians, thus giving her control over the regulations on the island. This would not be possible if she were not biracial/bicultural. Her European identity gives her the civility needed to work within the patriarchal system, while her Indian identity teaches her to engage in survival behavior such as hunting. Unca Eliza took pride in her ability to kill the goats on the island to sustain her life (63). The hunting skills of her dark aunt Alluca remain in her blood, even though she had been acculturated into English society. During her stay with the native Indians, she "sometimes amused [herself] in shooting with [her] bow and arrows" (119). Unca Eliza "can pursue ventures in Anglo culture that are traditionally reserved for men: education, hunting, [and] travel" because of her biracial identity, as she never fully becomes one identity or the other (Rex, 281). She consistently reemerges as a woman who can threaten the system of colonization due to her transgressive nature over the boundaries of gender roles.

In a direct feminist manner, Unca Eliza rejects the constraints of patriarchy by refusing marriage and having children. Prior to Unca Eliza's abandonment on the island, she notes that while she resided in Europe, "none touched my heart" and that she would "never marry a man who could not use a bow and arrow" (Winkfield, 50–51). Unca outwardly rejects the very gender roles prescribed to European women. She follows in her Amerindian mother's footsteps that it is "custom to be silent, or to speak what we think . . . the same right to declare our love as it has to" the male sex (43). She is exercising her right to love whom she chooses rather than be married based on the societal duty laid out by patriarchal notions. She is able to "subvert the subordination that . . . marriage attempted to press against women in the colonial period" because her identity is positioned in the liminal space between Indian and English (Rex, 264). This active choice to preserve both identities and openly exist in a liminal space frees Unca Eliza from patriarchy for most of the novel. However, one could argue that her decision to marry her cousin at the end is evident of her containment in patriarchy, yet the fact that they remained on the island with the Natives suggests otherwise. It seems that "she will be incorporated back into colonial and patriarchal discourses," since she marries her cousin even though he cannot use a bow and arrows (Rex, 285). She slightly bends into a European gender role, but her liminal identity as a bicultural female preserves her agency from full submersion. Her husband allows her to make the choice to remain on the island, thus granting her the power that would normally be in the hands of a man.

    While Unca Eliza's actions throughout the plot suggest that she crosses over the gender role lines, her ability to grant feminine authority to the story without a male guardian is the strongest testament to her ability to transcend oppressive powers.

In the beginning of the novel, the editor notes that "it ought to be a matter of indifference to him from what quarter or by what means, he receives it" (Winkfield, 33). The advertisement details that the voice of this novel regardless of it being female is worthy of being heard. Additionally, Unca Eliza argues that her narrative will have a permanent effect on the readers, unlike the "temporary effect" that adventures such as Robinson Crusoe will have on readers (106). Winkfield directly implies that the female voice is more authoritative and powerful than her male counterpart. Furthermore, she chooses to use her voice to convince the island natives that she is a powerful prophet. She states, "like a law-giver, I uttered precepts, and, like an orator, inculcated them with a voice magnified almost to the loudness of thunder" (86). She is a "woman daring to appropriate a very masculine task—telling her own story in her own voice" (Rex, 263). Not only does Unca Eliza have authorial power over the entire narrative, but she also grants herself the agency to be the female messiah for the natives. Her voice becomes an instrument for conversion and control of others. Unca Eliza's story is the first of its kind to be told from the perspective of the woman from beginning to end, and the first to grant a woman agency within a marginalized identity such as a biracial female.

Feminism is a large part of Unca Eliza's agency, but, most importantly, her agency is due to her position as an "other" resulting from her marginalized identity as a biracial and bicultural female. Her ability to cross into her otherness strongly affects her success in rejecting the traditional patriarchal gender roles. Colonization relied heavily on the conversion and acculturation of Amerindians into European culture. Many actively assimilated, but the otherness of being an outsider never fully disappears. This residual identity is what allows Unca Eliza to press against many of the patriarchal pressures of European society. For example, Unca Eliza's physical appearance and behaviors highlight her American identity that is an amalgamation of multiple cultures. First, she is "baptized by the name of Unca Eliza" (Winkfield, 47). She is named for both her Amerindian mother and provided an Anglican middle name which demonstrates "the melding of identities," thus granting her "an ominous, threatening power," as she is able to move back and forth between cultures (Rex, 234). A woman who has the power to cross boundaries threatens the patriarchal colonization of the New World because she is not fully subjected to the traditional European gender roles. Secondly, Unca Eliza's physical appearance exemplifies her liminal situation and multiplicity. She dresses oddly, "for [her] mother used to dress [her] in a kind of mixed habit, neither perfectly in the Indian, nor yet in the European taste" (Winkfield, 49). Unca Eliza wore European garments, but often adorned her body with precious stones and diamonds, often carrying a bow and arrow on her side. Winkfield writes herself as an "identity . . . of two distinct and supposedly diametrically opposed races, in which her literal in-between status. . . proves to be the most destabilizing and problematic element within the text" (Rex, 256). She purposely positions herself in a liminal space that makes it possible to break out of a confining role. Her mixed dress is a sign that she possesses the power to be more than one sort of person. She carries her histories with her and refuses to suppress her Indian traditions. In this nature, the other can destroy the patriarchal binary of male or female, and of Indian or European, in exchange for multiplicity. Unca Eliza has access to the traditional European female role and the free-spirited Indian role, thus granting her an agency that colonization attempted to thwart. The last space of otherness that Unca Eliza occupies is that of language. She "could already speak the Indian language as well as English, or with more fluency" (Winkfield, 50). Unca Eliza escapes the exclusive binary of only speaking one language and is able to survive on the island and in the New World due to her biracial identity. She is educated and able to remove herself from the constraints of marginalization by employing her otherness as part Amerindian in a way that grants her agency over her choices in society. This factor demonstrates that an "Indian woman who acculturated . . . could not entirely leave their Indianness behind" (Rex, 224).

Unca Eliza has a great deal of flexibility in her otherness as she can use the culture of her past alongside her present culture to form an identity that does not situate itself within the comforting expectations of Englishmen.

    The acculturation of Amerindian women into European colonization proved to be threatening if the woman learned to use her marginal position to cross over traditional gender boundaries. Unca Eliza utilized her mother's Indianness to survive on an island that required masculine strength. Her decision to go Native and abandon her learned European ways guided her until she was ready to reaccept pieces of the patriarchal society such as marrying her cousin. However, her liminal identity as a biracial and bicultural woman granted her agency that a European woman would not have access to. However, a question remains about Unca Eliza's agency: does she truly transcend traditional gender roles while trapped on the island or is it the hermit lifestyle that helps her survive?

Thoughts on Captivity Narratives

The fake Barbary captivity story *History of the Captivity and Sufferings of Mrs. Maria Martin* functions as a narrative account that brings together religious piety alongside Barbarian culture to show the importance of religion (in the eyes of those publishing this material). Considering that the editor made it clear that female captive stories were reborn in the 20th century as pulp romance, I would argue that the literature functions much in the way that Charlotte Temple functioned. The captivity story functions two ways: to prove the importance of religion for women and as a piece of political propaganda.

First, the story follows a woman who is taken captive to Algiers by Barbarians and survives with great stress. Not only does the story warn women of being too forthright, but there is also a strong theme toward religious piety. For example, the woman consistently states, "through the goodness of God" and "Oh Heavens!" to insinuate that the reasoning behind her survival during this kidnapping is the work of God (152). Moreover, this literature suggests to women that God protects women who are pious and stand against giving into men of other religions. There is another point in the piece that suggests that religious piety is the major function of the work. Upon her capture and transition to the apartment, a Turk comes in and tells her that God will rescue her from this place, so she does not have to convert from Christianity to Islam (153). It seems that the author is suggesting that Christianity must be preserved and women who follow in the footsteps of it will persevere. There is a hint that she would not survive the captivity if she were to succumb to the bashaw's desire to convert her to Islam.

Additionally, the literature functions as a piece of political propaganda for women and men reading it during the early half of American history. The notion that this woman comes from an upstanding family with the fortune to travel suggests that this piece would be used to inform citizens of the barbarian behavior that needs to be handled. The boat that she would board would be heading back to London, and the fact that England's imperialism was strong in North Africa points to the concept that the piece would convince citizens that their government, as a public service, must colonize these civilizations to avoid further captures.

Maternal Inheritance in *Breath, Eyes, Memory*

Breath, Eyes, Memory by Edwidge Danticat is an exemplary novel that explores the theme of maternal inheritance. The maternal inheritance featured throughout the novel provides an intriguing representation of motherhood and complicates our understanding of the standard definition of motherhood. This is most prevalent in the passage on pages 155–157 in chapter twenty-three. In this passage, Sofie is recounting the times that her mother tested her and then the narrative switches back into the present with Sofie think about her mother and Tante Atie being tested by her grandmother Ife. Sofie decides to ask her grandmother about the testing and why mothers choose to test their daughters. The conversation leads to a dialogue that introduces the idea of maternal inheritance and a mother's expected responsibilities for their daughter's innocence. Lastly, the passage ends with Ife apologizing for the trauma that she has caused Sofie.

The theme of maternal inheritance seeks to represent motherhood as an ideology passed down through the generations. Sofie's mother and grandmother, and perhaps all women before them, have continued to pass down the Haitian practices within motherhood, such as "testing" (Danticat, 155). For example, Sofie asks her grandmother, "Why do mothers do that?" and Grandme Ife replies with, "if your child is disgraced, you are disgraced" and mothers must keep their daughters pure "until they had husbands" (156). The practices within motherhood are designed to make good mothers and good daughters; Sofie learns from her mother and her grandmother that "good" mothers in Haiti are required to follow these practices and pass them down to their daughters, unless they would like to have "trash" for a daughter. In both instances, the ideology of motherhood is being passed down through the women even though it does not include successful practices. Interestingly, Sofie points out to Ife that the testing that she did on her daughters did not result in successful marriages and both of her daughters remain unmarried. I believe that the most important line is Ife stating, "The burden was not mine alone," to signal that this practice is shared by her ancestors and her descendants (156). It demonstrates that motherhood is represented as a concept that is passed down.

In addition to maternal inheritance representing motherhood as an ideology, the theme serves to complicate the definition of what the "good" mother is in Haitian culture. During this passage, Grandme Ife struggles with the conflict between adhering to testing in order to preserve a daughter's innocence and the emotional trauma that the process causes the daughter. It is clear that Ife believes that Sofie "must know that everything a mother does, she does for her child's own good," but there is a doubt in this statement since Ife says, "My heart weeps like a river" with regard to the trauma that she and Martine have caused Sofie (157). Ife knows that she is supposed to keep her daughter's innocence preserved through testing, yet she knows that it causes severe trauma as well. Thus, a "good" mother must learn to be okay with "the burden" of hurting their daughters to maintain their status as a "good" mother (156). I would argue that this statement on motherhood is designed to highlight that motherhood, through practice and ideology, can be messy and not necessarily a singularly loving role. Mothers must adhere to their practices in order to teach their daughters to be "good" mothers regardless of the trauma it may cause.

The Disruption of Filial Piety in *Charlotte Temple*

Early American literature revels in the delicate balance between young adults following their parents' commands for their children's futures and the decision to forgo such a demand. The filial piety in many eighteenth-century seduction novels lends itself to show a moral story for young women, but what about the outcomes for men who choose to disobey this set code? Moreover, does this choice then lead to the success or failure of the woman that a man chooses to disregard his duty for? It seems that there may be a gray area in the decision to act against patrilineal obligations. In Susana Rowson's *Charlotte Temple*, the men of the novel, particularly Charlotte Temple's father and her seducer, act out of societal standards and follow their intuitions. Mr. Temple marries Lucy Eldridge and Montraville elopes (without marrying) with Charlotte Temple. The outcomes are starkly different with Mr. Temple's abandonment of filial duty leading to a successful marriage, while Montraville's decision ultimately leads to the death of Charlotte Temple. The sub-plot of Mr. Temple's decision juxtaposed with Montraville's decision signals that one's intention when choosing to ignore filial piety is critical to the outcome of making such a decision. While Susanna Rowson's *Charlotte Temple* consistently condones filial piety through tone, figurative language, and character outcomes, and there is an understated argument that a man with the right intentions can prosper by forgoing such a duty, while a man who does not carry good intentions is unacceptable and will end up in ruin.

    The narrator's tone towards abandoning filial piety with respect to the intentions of Mr. Temple and Montraville demonstrate that only good intentions are worthy of such abandonment, otherwise, a man should oblige to his duties. Both men are described positively prior to their choices in ignoring filial piety for a woman of their choice. For example, Mr. Temple "had a heart open" and "his feelings [were] warm" as a young man who wants to help others and marry a woman that he truly loves (Rowson, 41 & 49). Moreover, Montraville is similarly described as a man "generous in his disposition" and "good-natured to a fault" (61). The tone for each man is warm, as they are described as worthy men with good intentions and willing to contribute to society. This tone remains the same for Mr. Temple as he proves that his intentions for Lucy Eldridge are true, while the tone turns negative for Montraville as his intentions for Charlotte Temple are proven rash and untrue. Mr. Temple "offers his heart and hand to Lucy Eldridge" and marries her even though she does not have as large fortune as his father wishes, and he commits to supporting her and her father regardless of this, which demonstrates that he truly desires to take care of her (52). Their union, although against filial piety, is "attended by Love and Hymen" and endures "many years of uninterrupted felicity" because Mr. Temple treats Lucy with respect and honor. He did not falter in his intentions, unlike Montraville. Montraville, who swoons over Charlotte, does not follow through and thus the tone toward his character and actions changes drastically. Montraville forces Charlotte into eloping, but then his feelings for her dissipate and he turns to another woman (69). It is revealed that Montraville "did not design to marry her" when they got to America (78). Montraville is emotionally tortured throughout the latter half of the novel for his behavior toward Charlotte and upon her death, he suffers with grief for the rest of his life. The narrator clearly disapproves of lusting intentions and argues that a man should not contradict his filial duty unless his intentions are true and do not hurt the woman involved. Thus, this tonal contradiction between Mr. Temple and Montraville supports the decision to abandon filial piety only if the intentions are good and the man honors his promises; otherwise, a man should obey his patrilineal obligations.

While tone is important, the language used to describe Mr. Temple's and Montraville's filial obligations and their convictions developed towards their duties further highlights the acceptance of a man's decision to forgo those obligations depending on their intentions for the woman. Both Montraville's and Mr. Temple's fathers had expectations for the type of woman that their son would marry. For example, Mr. Temple's father did not have a large fortune and advised his son to marry Miss Weatherby for her large fortune (50). On the other hand, Montraville's father had a large fortune, but taught his son to earn his own wealth and then seek a wife that he could care for in the end (63). Both men are expected to fulfill their patrilineal duties, yet each man goes against these expectations for love or lust. Based on these intentions, the reader can see the language morph to demonstrate that poor intentions are no reason for abandoning filial piety. For example, Mr. Temple plans to "marry where the feelings of his heart should direct him" and does so when he chooses to abandon his father and pursue Lucy Eldridge (41). His honorable word led to "Plenty . . . and . . . Prudence" to be at their side as they established a life for themselves (52). The two live happily together without the blessing of Mr. Temple's father, as the personifications of the words indicate that the decision granted them a worthy life. Alternatively, Montraville "couldn't bear to marry a girl he didn't love" and abandons his filial piety and Charlotte Temple after promising her his honor and love to marry a woman of higher fortune (61–62). Upon realizing that he made a mistake, Montraville refers to himself as a "villain" for rushing into an affair with Charlotte (84). Both men follow their hearts, but the intentions within that heart are not well thought out for Montraville as he forces Charlotte into eloping, only to meet a woman that he truly falls in love with upon arriving to America. Moreover, he ignores his father for lusting after Charlotte and leaving her in despair as his father asked him not to. His abandonment of filial piety is unacceptable and the language points to this as intentions are not fulfilled; he rushes into a promise that he cannot keep. In Mr. Temple's situation, he abandons filial duty that is superficial for an honorable marriage to a woman that adores his gracious heart. He keeps his promises and demonstrates that his intentions were worthy of her hand and ignoring his father's requests.

The outcomes of each man's decision to forgo filial piety demonstrates that abandoning such obligation is only acceptable when a man's intentions are true and he follows through with his promises. As in the beginning of each man's courtship, promises are made to these women, but the lack of follow-through and the meaning of their intentions lead to an outcome that argues for the acceptance of adhering to filial piety. Mr. Temple chooses to marry Lucy Eldridge against his father's request and they share "many years" of love and happiness before the event of their daughter Charlotte; however, their love and duty to one another prevailed throughout life regardless of his choice (125). Although they lost their daughter to the misfortune of Montraville, they gained a granddaughter who they could raise for the poor young woman. Mr. Temple's good intentions in the beginning of his relationship with Lucy and the positive outcome of his abandonment of filial piety demonstrate that it is not always wise to listen to one's parent. Rather than choosing a superficial wife for fortune, his choice to follow his heart was an acceptable reason for doing so. Unfortunately, the same cannot be said for Montraville. Montraville's quick-minded elopement and lust for Charlotte led to a terrible outcome for him and for her. He is a "feeble" man that dishonored Charlotte and himself in his selfish act of seduction (84). After Montraville left Charlotte alone at the cottage to be with Julia Franklin, the fates of both characters were in despair. Charlotte Temple dies in childbirth and Montraville falls into an "obstinate delirium" which he never fully overcomes as he regretted his actions toward Charlotte Temple for the rest of his life (122–124). Both young characters end in demise because Montraville did not fulfill his filial piety, nor did he abandon it with good intentions for the future of himself and for Charlotte.

  The sub-plot of Mr. Temple juxtaposed against the overlying plot of Montraville seducing Charlotte Temple is poignant in outlining what makes it acceptable to abandon the ever-present notion of filial piety. Filial piety is the central theme to the novel, yet the characters continuously defy it and find themselves successful or in total despair depending on the originations of such defiance. Mr. Temple defies his father's desire for a marriage based on financial advantage for a harmonious marriage with the less-privileged Lucy Eldridge. His positive intentions for the young woman in his haste to marry her and their successful marriage argue for the acceptability to go against certain obligations. Moreover, Montraville's irrational lust and seduction of Charlotte Temple and his choice to abandon her for another woman illustrate that choosing to ignore filial piety for poor intentions with a woman is unacceptable and results in demise. This black and white distinction between the small conflict of Mr. Temple and the overall plot of Montraville argues that filial obedience can have a gray area for men who are willing to be true to the woman they fall in love with. However, Montraville's destruction of Charlotte Temple through his defiance of patrilineal obligation leads the reader to wonder whether this is a statement on gender politics or a real warning for young women against men who do not have trustworthy intentions.

On Philosophy and History

Role of Virginity and Independence of Women in Classical Athens Depicted in the Goddesses: Artemis, Athena, and Aphrodite

The direct democracy of classical Athens was far from all-inclusive: Athenian women had little participation in the public, political, or societal sphere of the great city-state. The status of Athenian women was deplorable and secluded to the private sphere within the oikos (household). Athenian women were not regarded as citizens, and they were expected to maintain virginity prior to marriage and then become a wife and a mother. Any role outside of these positions was considered unacceptable. This disembodiment of female agency and the expected behavior of Athenian women by society can be seen in the depictions of the Greek goddesses Artemis, Athena, and Aphrodite. The three goddesses stood for the importance Athenians placed on virginity and marriage; the virgin goddesses were able to behave outside of female expectations (however, they lost their sexuality), while the married goddess lost her ability to perform within the public sphere. In this culture, the importance placed on virginity not only kept women chaste, but it was also a testament to the honor of men. Moreover, the seclusion and objectification of women as a tool to aid Athenian men further prevented women from being independent. The creation of goddesses that surround female virginity and societal expectations mirrored the political and societal regulations and expectations created for Athenian women during classical Greece. During the classical period of Greece within the city-state of Athens, the depiction of (and importance placed on) goddesses Artemis, Athena, and Aphrodite, with respect to female virginity and independence, directly mirrored the political and societal perspective of Athenian women, thereby highlighting classical Athens' need to have patriarchal power over female agency.

    The societal and political expectations of Athenian women positioned them in the private sphere and demanded them be either virgins or wives. This extremely narrow space of existence pressed women into seclusion, away from the public sphere and solely into the domestic realm. For example, most Athenian women never left their homes and many "seldom crossed the threshold of their own front doors," as any contact with men outside of the oikos threatened their chastity and family's reputation (Cohen, "Seclusion," 4). This seclusion became more prevalent in Athens "during the fifth century . . . when democratic ideals of liberty were institutionalized" (Katz, 73). The seclusion of women and the creation of democracy for Athenian men allowed for the partitioning of the roles of women to be primarily focused on their virginity as a critical factor in their ability to be married into other Greek families, as well as to create the patriarchal gender roles that forced women into specific societal behaviors. Furthermore, Sue Blundell points out that "it was of utmost importance . . . that their daughters are virgins . . . but [of] equal importance that women should marry and give birth," which further illustrates that women had two options within the political and societal structure of Athens during the classical period (25). Virginity was critical to the societal movement of Greek families, as only a legitimate Athenian citizen (i.e. a male) could take part in property inheritance and business, hence the importance placed on chastity by men. Athenian democracy dictated that women perform roles that served Athenian men. Thus, the depiction of female goddesses who boldly protected virginity or performed as the perfect wife, provided women pictorials of Athenian values that would help maintain the patriarchal society and keep women from interjecting into the public arena.

These female roles: virginity and marriage (and women performing correctly both societally and politically within these boundaries) are depicted in the goddesses Athena, Artemis, and Aphrodite, yet, none of these goddesses have full agency, as a component of femaleness has been stripped from them in order to display the importance of virginity or of being a mother and/or wife. First, Athena, the goddess of war and wisdom is portrayed as a warrior and as an androgynous figure who possesses feminine and masculine characteristics. Perhaps, the most important characteristic is her decision to remain a "dedicated virgin" (Blundell, 28). Her vigilance to uphold her virginity further enhances the expected behavior within the patriarchal society. By choosing to remain a virgin, Athena demonstrates how important it is for Athenian women to remain chaste until she is betrothed. She never allows the reputation of her father, Zeus, to be destroyed. However, Athena chooses to "reject the roles of marriage and motherhood which most Greek men saw as fundamental to a women's existence" (Blundell, 26). To maintain both female and male activities and traits, she must give up being a wife or mother. She is able to free herself of the societal expectations of being a woman trapped indoors and transcend the lines between public and private by acting in war and on a political level (e.g. assisting Perseus defeat the Gorgons), but she loses her sexuality in exchange for this "freedom." It would seem that Athena would be a threat to the expected behaviors for Athenian women, but it is her position as a woman and as a weaver that keep her from being a threat to the patriarchal structure. Although she possesses masculine traits, she is at the heart of the home. Xenophon points out that Athenian women have "authority over weaving," and, likewise, Cohen argues that women are associated with the duties of the home (Cohen, 5–6). Moreover, in many Greek stories, Athena often gains permission from Zeus to partake in male-centered activities, thus highlighting the same experience that Greek women dealt with each day, as no woman was independent of a man. Athena's inability to gain full independence and her domestic situation as a weaver depict the same political and social roles of Athenian women. Women were to remain virgins until they were married and were involved in domestic tasks as adults, regardless of their position as wife or otherwise.

    In addition to Athena, Artemis, the goddess of hunting, virginity, and childbirth, forcefully protects her virginity, thus demonstrating Greece's view on its women remaining chaste. A woman's ability to remain a virgin defined a man's honor during this period (Cohen, "Law," 140). Her choice to defend the attribute that Athenian society tells women to value most provides an adequate account for the women of Athens during the classical period. Athenian women remained indoors and did not speak to men from the outside, nor interact with men who entered their homes. In this, women fall prey to the male control of women within society. Interestingly, Artemis remains a virgin forever, yet serves as the goddess of childbirth, an act that she never experiences. According to Blundell, Artemis "defends her chastity vigorously" from Actaean and "expresses her antipathy to the married state" (31). Her attempt to thwart sexual acts and marriage liberate her from the traditional roles of women. Since she never truly becomes a mature woman, she is able to participate in masculine activities, such as hunting. She is able to function within the male societal sphere, yet she is not fully granted the wonderments of being a woman who becomes a wife and mother. Her inability to be a sexual female is a display of the disruption of female agency within Greek society. Women cannot be free within a sexual marriage (as an independent woman), nor can she be free as a dedicated virgin who never becomes a full woman. Moreover, Artemis maintains her "sexual purity," which is "guarded and demonstrated to the community," as a coveted role for women to adhere to in society (Cohen, "Seclusion," 6). Her adherence to chastity and her participation in childbirth are seen in the treatment of virginity and motherhood in Athenian culture—they are the only features of a good woman's life. Artemis is an exemplary figure for Athenian women as she provides the morality of being a virgin and the importance of bearing children due to her roles as a goddess.

    While Athena and Artemis are virgins who exemplify the role of virginity in Greek society, the goddess of love, Aphrodite, depicts the perfect Athenian woman as she fulfills both roles as a wife and as a mother. She is wife to Hephaestus and mother to Eros. Athenian code dictated that women were to be shifted from one kyrios (guardian) to another, most often a husband. Much like Athenian women,

Aphrodite was forced to marry her husband by Zeus as an attempt to deflect any fighting that would erupt to ascertain her (due to her beauty). Her role as an "Athenian wife" grants her "respect," unlike women who are not married to a man. (Katz, 74). She is subjected to the same patriarchal treatment as Athenian women, thus providing an example for all women that this is the route which all women must take to maintain virtue and reputation. Moreover, Aphrodite comes "under male domination" by bearing a child with a man that she does not love because that was the expected societal responsibility for Greek women during the classical period (Blundell, 44). As a Greek woman, Aphrodite "must obey a man," as they have total control over a woman's life, especially with respect to marriage (Katz, 75). The behavior mirrors that of Athenian woman and demonstrates how women were transferred from one home to the next in order to keep them guarded from the outside world. Not only does Aphrodite portray the ideal female role under Athenian society, but she also marries as a political step to avoid conflict. This instance depicts the importance of marrying whomever is chosen for an Athenian woman so that she may fulfill her societal and political duty to her people.

      The mythology of all three goddesses, Athena, Artemis, and Aphrodite, not only depict the roles designed for Athenian women, but they also demonstrate the patriarchal removal of female agency from these women and highlight Greece's perspective on the function of women within society. Each goddess is empowered with some form of female agency; however, she is not granted complete agency over her sexuality or independence due to societal constraints dictated by the Athenian patriarchy. Athena and Artemis must remain virgins since they choose not to marry and have children, while Aphrodite becomes a mother and wife but cannot remove herself from the private, feminine sphere. Athena and Artemis represent Athenian women who are virgins and demonstrate that "female honor largely involves sexual purity" and that "unbridled female sexuality" must be restrained (Cohen, 140). Since the two women do not get married, they must remain in total control of their bodies, much like the women of Athens. Athenian woman had no room to maneuver within this expectation. Women were to remain virgins until marriage. Female sexuality had to be restrained through chastity or through marriage, since women were regarded as tools to reproduce heirs that would later inherit a fortune (if it were available). Athenian law mandated that "[a] woman had no independent existence" (Blundell, 114). The goddesses and Athenian women did not control their bodies or decisions; rather, they were used politically to produce male citizens and socially to maintain the household for their husbands. Ultimately, Athenian women lived "as a species of slavery" that "implicitly relegates [them] to an entirely passive role in patriarchal society" (Katz, 76 and 79). Athenian women lived in seclusion for much of their lives and emulated the qualities of being a virgin, much like Athena and Artemis, but ultimately moving into the role as mother and wife, similarly to Aphrodite.

  The Athenian democracy did not include rights for women, nor did it provide them anything but patriarchal dominion that dictated the roles of their lives. The patriarchal society placed significant importance on virginity and marriage because political laws only permitted Athenian citizens to inherit property and fortune. Thus, women were expected to remain chaste until marriage and then serve as a tool for men within society. The mythological goddesses Athena, Artemis, and Aphrodite serve as female models that exemplify either the importance of virginity or of being an Athenian mother and wife. The goddesses give insight into the societal and political expectations of Athenian women to function within the patriarchal parameters of Greek society. Moreover, the women further highlight the lack of female agency granted to the goddesses and the females of Athens, as a woman must remain chaste or get married to function within society. Women were expected to remain in the private sphere, hidden away from the male population in order to preserve their honor. The creation of goddesses who either possessed virginity with more freedom or marriage with more honor, seems to be used to demonstrate to Greek women the roles that they were expected to perform and the ramifications of not abiding by the stringent laws of society. The mirroring of the Athenian female roles with the goddesses allowed classical Athens's democracy to maintain control over the population and participation of women at all levels of society. Does the seclusion of Athenian women and enslavement of them into marginalized roles truly allow the society to work properly, or was it the start of Athens's downfall?

Knowledge in sixteenth/seventeenth Century Europe: A Departure from Aristotelian Scholasticism to Rationalism Based on the Authorities of Religion, Experience, and Reason

The scientific, intellectual, and political expansions that occurred in Europe during the 16th and 17th centuries invoked many philosophers to develop claims and methods for determining truth and knowledge. Sixteenth century thinking was marked by anti-Aristotelian arguments, as well as the rebirth of skepticism due to the religious reformations and political transformations occurring throughout Europe. For example, Michele de Montaigne of France published "On Experience" in *Essays* in 1562, which stakes his claim for knowledge in deep skepticism and seeks to show that tradition, reason, or religion do not provide society with knowledge. Montaigne's humanist education and the Wars of Religion that occurred during his lifetime influenced the thinking of *Essays*. Following Montaigne, French philosopher René Descartes published *Discourse on Method* in 1637 and *Meditations on First Philosophy* in 1641, which is Descartes's rationalistic method on gaining and understanding knowledge/truth. While the books examine the method for truth, the arguments stand as a response to Aristotelian Scholasticism and the Inquisition of Galileo during the Scientific Revolution. Descartes philosophy inspired Cartesian circles throughout Europe, from which Benedict Spinoza, a Jewish-Dutch philosopher from Amsterdam, was spurred to publish the *Theological-Political Treatise* in 1670. The main purpose was to demonstrate that thinkers had the right to philosophize without the interference of religion, which was heavy-handed due to the disputes of the political control over religion. All three thinkers give authority to religion, reason, and/or experience in their claim to knowledge, as well as discuss the value of relying on the tradition established by ancient thinkers, such as Plato and Aristotle. Moreover, the way in which these scholars conceived the quest for knowledge changes in response to the political and religious influences aim to control philosophy. The claim to knowledge slowly transform from remarkably skeptical to rationally methodical as time progresses from Montaigne to Descartes to Spinoza. The rapid expansion of ideas combined with religious and political schisms in Europe during the sixteenth and seventeenth centuries sparked the minds of René Descartes, Benedict Spinoza, and Michel de Montaigne to make claims for knowledge through authorities such as religion, reason, and experience; each thinker further evaluates the importance of tradition and ancient texts in regard to knowledge.

René Descartes, Michel de Montaigne, and Benedict Spinoza asserted their knowledge claims based on skepticism or rationalism; furthermore, each thinker refutes the tradition of ancient texts in exchange for a progressive method for gaining knowledge. Sixteenth century thinker Montaigne philosophizes on gaining knowledge by refuting the ancients and establishing himself as a skeptic. For example, Montaigne states, "I would rather understand myself well by self-study than by reading Cicero" in his statement against relying on ancient text (Montaigne, 354). Montaigne refutes the scholastic notion that to understand and gain knowledge one must read, which can be attributed to the religious schisms caused by Luther during Montaigne's lifetime. Experience becomes the basis for his philosophy on epistemology. Moreover, Montaigne claims it is impossible to know with certainty, but what people must "know" is determined by one's experiences rather than through reasoning or religion (343). Experience is the key to his knowledge, as each individual possesses only his own senses of life through experience. On the other hand, Descartes agrees with the refutation of tradition and of ancient thinkers; he develops a method for gaining knowledge through reason. Descartes refutes the ancients claiming that society is "making themselves less knowledgeable than if they abstained from studying [ancient philosophers]" (Descartes, 39). He rejects Aristotle's syllogisms arguing that they are "harmful" and "the ancients . . . seem to be of no use" as they do not understand the current social setting (10). This defiance against tradition fits his philosophy that relies on hyperbolic doubt and breaking down current notions completely to find truth (18). Descartes's claim on knowledge rests in certainty. If an idea is placed in his mind and he can reason it based on hyperbolic doubt that it did not come from the senses, then it is possible that the knowledge exists. However, Descartes makes it clear that one can never be certain that the idea is pure or exists. Much like Descartes, Spinoza subscribes to reason as a claim for knowledge, however he argues that he knew the ways to attain knowledge and that he knew all truths based on deductive reasoning. He argues, "our mind possesses the power to form such notions from this alone—the it objectively contains within itself the nature of God and participates in it" (Spinoza, 14). Spinoza claims that knowledge exists within the mind and that the mind has the power to know all that is needed to be known as reasoning and God (or nature) provides it. As Descartes and Montaigne reject tradition,

Spinoza rejects the ancient texts and tradition in addition to the imposition of theology within philosophy. He states, "[I am] utterly amazed that men should want to subject reason . . . the ancient words which may well have been adulterated with malicious intent." (Spinoza, 188). Much of his discussion revolves around the separation of theology and reason, while suggesting that the ancient texts are unreliable to progressive thinking, as they have been passed through too many hands.

Each philosopher's epistemology claims rest under the authority of reason, religion, or experience; both Descartes and Spinoza argue that reason is the main authority over knowledge, while Montaigne counter-argues that hyperbolic reasoning interferes with the attainment of knowledge (which of course he believes is merely subjective to the individual). Descartes argues that only way to know truth is through the rational mind and not through the senses. For example, he uses an anecdote of solid wax and melting wax, stating that the rational mind knows that they are the same, but the senses are deceiving, as they will register the two forms of wax as different substances (Descartes, 69). He concludes that "by the intellect alone . . . I manifestly know that nothing can be perceived . . . more evidently than my own mind" (69). He reasons that one must let go of all preconceived truths and allow absolute truths to filter into the mind from the ground up. Moreover, he positions himself to believe that reason dictates that all ideas have partial truth to underline his hyperbolic doubt in believing that anything is an absolute truth (unless granted by God), thus he creates the method to seek knowledge (22). Descartes's method is to reason an find truths, one must abandon all former notions and reevaluate every idea that comes into the mind over time. Similar to Descartes, Spinoza, who published thirty years later, developed a philosophy on knowledge that includes similar rationality that reason is critical to knowledge. However, he went further to claim that he knows how to attain all knowledge and in fact, he knows everything. His belief that persons have the power to possess ideas within their minds without significant doubt separates his rational perspective from

Descartes's skeptical perspective. Spinoza believes that "reason . . . reigns over the domain of the truth" and "no spirit other than reason gives testimony about the truth and certainty" (Spinoza, 190 and 193). Spinoza reasons that knowledge can be attained by disregarding all former testimony, then reasoning that an idea that is attributed to the divine essence can be applied to all ideas that stem from that idea. Unlike Descartes and Spinoza, Montaigne argues against reason as the main authority over knowledge. According to Montaigne, "a man of great ability will not be satisfied [with knowledge] . . . there is no end to our investigations" (Montaigne, 348). Furthermore, he claims that reason teaches "men to increase their doubts" and "experience shows us that all these interpretations dissipate the truth and destroy it" (346). His perspective on reason is that it hinders a man's ability to gain personal knowledge through experience and that the hyperbolic doubt in Descartes method and Spinoza's all-knowing perspectives over-analyze the simplicity of the individuality of knowledge. Montaigne holds reason in high authority over understanding life, yet he favors a more sense-based reason that factors in self-study rather than a more generalized version of knowledge that Descartes and Spinoza seek.

As reason takes predominant authority in the philosophers claims to knowledge, religion (more importantly, the existence of God) is important to Montaigne, Spinoza, and Descartes, but in much different ways. In *Discourse on Method*, Descartes uses reason to extrapolate that the existence of God is perfect. God is the origination of all knowledge that is in the mind. Thus, in combination with reason, Descartes places great authority on religion with having knowledge as he claims, "I could not obtain it from myself . . . this idea had been placed in me by a nature truly more perfect than I was . . . that it was God. (Descartes, 19). Descartes recognizes that knowledge is divine and that the truths within him are infinite, much as the God that he believes puts ideas into his mind. Moreover, Descartes reasons that without knowing God, one cannot know anything at all, as it is this pure substance, God, which has the power to give men knowledge. Spinoza agrees with Descartes's writing, "For everything that we understand clearly and distinctly is dictated to us . . . by the idea of God" (Spinoza, 14). Spinoza deems knowledge divine and natural, but unlike Descartes, he argues that theology "deem[s] it impious to have doubts . . . of those who have handed down the sacred books" (Spinoza, 188). This philosophy claims that theology should not reprimand philosophy for interpreting and analyzing the Sacred Scriptures for better understanding of that knowledge. Spinoza was under scrutiny during his epistemological development and he argues that God's word should be able to be reasoned by men, rather than to follow the reasoning of the church. Thus, Spinoza agrees that God is responsible for knowledge as men could access God's word, but it is reason that is required to understand the knowledge as truth. Likewise, Montaigne parallels Spinoza's argument that philosophers should be allowed to interpret the Scripture without the interference of the church translating the text first. Furthermore, Montaigne fights against religion (not God), attempting to persuade men into submission against their own refutes on knowledge stating, "And those men who think they can lessen . . . our disputes . . . by referring us to . . . the Bible are deluding themselves" (Montaigne, 344). Montaigne never attributes gaining knowledge to God because he does not think that knowledge can be owned, but he does argue that experience gives one specified knowledge based on those experiences. Here, Montaigne is throwing the Sola Scriptura back into the face of theology, as he does not believe that religious texts can be of use to the self-study process without a personal interpretation. In the case of religion, each thinker agrees that religion hinders the process of attaining knowledge because it beckons society to believe solely in the words of the church rather than in reasoning God's relationship to knowledge.

The authority of experience wavers in influence on the claim to knowledge, as Montaigne believes it is the main authority on knowledge, while Descartes and Spinoza believe that experience alone cannot provide truths. As Montaigne is skeptical of owning knowledge, he formulated his philosophy around experience through self-study. He opens his essay, "On Experience" with the phrase, "When reason fails us, we make use of experience" to illustrate his argument that knowledge is unique to everyone's life experience (Montaigne, 343). Reason should include experience as a diverse form of itself. His skepticism on knowledge stems from this core point that knowledge is not universal and that it is reliant on one's sensory perception of the truth. Furthermore, he cites experience as an authority on truth because he subscribes to sense-based reasoning, claiming that, "I judge myself only by actual sensations, not by reasoning" (381). "On Experience" highlights a number of Montaigne's personal experiences to demonstrate that he likes wine a certain way and believes that to be his knowledge on wine, but he is aware that a person in another country will know wine differently. While Montaigne's experience stems from the sensory, Descartes perspective on experience is situated in reason. Much like Montaigne, Descartes abandoned his schooling and traveled the world open to all experiences in his search for truth (Descartes, 5). As he develops hyperbolic doubt and certainty as his method for claiming knowledge, he abandons the senses to analyze all experiences through reason. He states, "[I am] spending my whole life cultivating my reason and advancing, as far as I could, in the knowledge of the truth" (Descartes, 15). This thought demonstrates that there is a change from Montaigne to Descartes in regard to how knowledge is attained. Montaigne is specific in making knowledge personal, while Descartes develops a method for generalized knowledge that all of society could have through reason. Descartes's experiences were processed with extreme reason to rid his mind of any deceiving truths that may have been put there by something other than God. Beyond Montaigne and Descartes, Spinoza develops a place for knowledge within authority, but, like Descartes, he did not place it in high authority. Spinoza believes that men "must live and conserve themselves . . . before they can learn the true rationale of living" (Spinoza, 196). Thus, Spinoza, who values a hybridized version of experience taking in the senses and reason, argues that experience is important to understanding knowledge, but one must have a hard grasp on living an obedient life before they can rely on experience for truth.

Descartes, Spinoza, and Montaigne have epistemological claims that are situated with skepticism and rationalism. During the sixteenth and seventeenth centuries, these thinkers witnessed remarkable religious and political schisms that forced them to turn to reason, religion, or experience to form ideas on how men have and gain knowledge. While Montaigne differs from Spinoza and Descartes by formulating that knowledge cannot be known due to the diversity between men's experiences, he did allow reason to have a lot of authority on the development of what a man could know of himself. Montaigne values the senses to know, while Spinoza and Descartes chose hyperbolic doubt and reason to understand knowledge. In part, this shift between the senses and rationality could be caused by the religious strife that Montaigne faced and the religious-political prosecution that Spinoza and Descartes faced during their times.

More importantly, it is clear that many thinkers in Europe during the sixteenth and seventeenth centuries abandoned tradition and the heavy reliance on the ancient texts. Moreover, all three men relied on God for knowledge or guidance, but each refuted the traditional concept of theology controlling the interpretations of God's word. While all three men differ significantly in their epistemological philosophies, all men seemed to be searching for the key to grant men the freedom to philosophize for them and to allow society to understand knowledge without the interference of the political persuasion of religion.

The Visions of European Unity

Europe found itself disunited after a long string of devastating wars. As the countries began to rebuild and restructure alliances, efforts were made to unite Western Europe as a whole. As the European Community became a passionate goal of many nations, the thoughts and visions of a united Europe exploded from the minds of many influential European politicians. The thoughts of British Prime Minister Margaret Thatcher were presented in "Speech to the College of Europe, Bruges," in 1988, revealing her loosened ideas of what a united Europe would look like. Moreover, Jean Monnet, a French politician and founding father of European unity, penned his visions in "A Ferment for Change," while his counterpart Charles de Gaulle, former French Prime Minister, expressed his ideas in "Europe." Lastly, Jacques Delors, another French politician, spoke of his perspective on a united Europe in his speech "A Necessary Union," which was presented to the College of Europe in Bruges one year after Thatcher had delivered her ideas to the crowd. Each politician maintained a strong sense of what should be entailed in the European Union/European Community, including ideas/suggestions on free enterprise, national sovereignty, involvement with outside nations, and the inclusion of Germany in the unification. The structuring and position of the European Community (now the European Union, or the EU) with respect to a free market, national sovereignty, international relations, and the inclusion of Germany were largely decided and envisioned by Margaret Thatcher, Charles de Gaulle, Jacques Delors, and Jean Monnet.

The vision of a free market on the continent as a requirement for success was envisioned by Thatcher, Monnet, and Delors, while De Gaulle deemed it a hindrance to the success of European unity. The allowance of a free market would allow countries within the Community to freely (or at least with little financial impact) import and export goods with countries outside of the Community. Margaret Thatcher stated that "free enterprise within a framework of law brings better results" than one that does not allow for it at all (Thatcher, 1988). Moreover, Monnet agreed, stating, "I am thinking of world agriculture . . . the need for growing trade between Japan and the United States and Europe together" would build a more successful, unified Europe (Monnet, 209). Similarly, Delors, while less open to a free market, agreed that "we need to give countries that depend on exports for survival access to our markets," in the hopes that a semi-free market would boost the economy and not devastate smaller countries with mounds of debt incurred by high tariffs (Delors, 1989). On the other hand, De Gaulle did not find a free market appealing to the creation of the European Union. He stated that the Six should "establish an external tariff," and he refused to join the European Community if this tariff was not a part of the plan (De Gaulle, 186). Eventually, there was a lower tariff in place, however it was with due diligence that it was put in place.

In addition to ideas on a free market, the politicians of Europe were divided in terms of the European Community dissolving the national structure of the countries or maintaining national sovereignty. The anti-socialistic perspective of Thatcher was clear in her speech, stating that the Union should maintain the cultures of all of the nations (Thatcher, 1988). Moreover, she claimed that "willing and active cooperation between independent sovereign states is the best way to build a successful European Community," while suppressing nationhood "would be highly damaging" (Thatcher, 1988). She felt that dissolving these cultures would lead to dissent and a spiral back into another war between the countries. Monnet was an advocate for national sovereignty, as well. Monnet believed that the nations should remain separate but follow certain rules within the Community that benefited all of the nations' future success. He stated that "common rules applied by joint institutions give each a responsibility for the effective working of the community as a whole," but this does not require sacrificing one's nationalism or pride (Monnet, 206). Monnet was concerned that France's pride would be tarnished by any dissolution, as he did not think that the country had fully recovered from the perils of World War II. On the other hand, De Gaulle and Delors fought for a federalist Union that brought all nations under one contract, rather than maintain national sovereignty. De Gaulle stated, "my policy therefore aimed at the setting up of a concert of European States which in developing all sorts of ties between them would increase their interdependence and solidarity" (De Gaulle, 171). Likewise, Delors claimed that "the need for a European power capable of tackling the problems of our age . . . would uphold the values of freedom and solidarity" (Delors, 56–57). Both men desired a tighter ruling of the European countries in order to maintain control over political, social, and economical institutions that kept the continent functioning. Furthermore, the men wanted to be at the same global level as the United States, Japan, and Russia at that time. With the development of the European Union, the nations maintained their sovereignty; however, a large developed parliament style group was developed to govern the laws of the EU.

As the nations decided to maintain national sovereignty and a partially free market, the countries had to decide what their involvement with external countries such as Britain and the United States would be like. Globalization became a major topic between the politicians. Anti-federalists Thatcher and Monnet envisioned a European Union that was strongly involved with foreign countries across the Atlantic and not located on the continent. Thatcher was quick to develop an idea for the Union that involved strong ties with the global economy. She stated that the European Community "should not be protectist," rather the Community should strengthen the ties with the United States (and other nations) in order to protect Europe and open it up to a large economic market (Thatcher, 1988). In the same vein, Monnet agreed, claiming that "the creation of a united Europe brings this nearer by making it possible for America and Europe to act as partners" instead of adversaries or competitors (Monnet, 209). Monnet saw these ties as imperative to increasing the economic output of the countries of the

Union. As a French politician, Monnet greatly considered the induction of Great Britain into the Community, as well. While many leaders did not want Great Britain to join the Union, Monnet saw it as a requirement for European success. He stated, "we must make every effort" to include Britain, "she will contribute to the success of the community" (Monnet, 208). The visions of De Gaulle were in opposition of extending an arm to the United States or to Great Britain being involved in the unification of the continent. With respect to Great Britain and the United States, De Gaulle stated, "to prevent certain others; in particular Great Britain, from dragging the west into an Atlantic system, which would be totally incompatible with a European Europe" (De Gaulle, 171–172). This resonates with his staunch federalist view. He wanted the European Community to benefit only those on the continent, considering any country not on the continent to be disbarred from any involvement within that tight federalist creation.

    Moreover, the European Community had to decide whether Germany would be made a part of the Union. After the disaster of World War II, it was difficult for many nations to accept Germany as a European country. However, there were concerns about including Germany as a European nation, because then their dissent could be recreated. Monnet was strong in stating that Germany must be a part of the Union because its people must be forgiven (De Gaulle, 202). Likewise, De Gaulle stated that "she should form an integral part of the organized system" in the hopes that the country could be put back together and function as a member of the Union (De Gaulle, 173). Additionally, Thatcher and Delors strongly agreed that Germany should maintain the current treaties against its reconstruction, yet the country should be inducted into the Community, as it has always been a European country. Through the unification of Europe, Germany was included in the unification process.

The European Community was created with many of these thoughts and visions in mind. Each politician shared his/her view as to what the Community should entail. Over years, the European Union was formed with every bit of equality possible within a union that spreads across national borders. There came a balance between the free market and the use of a tariff. The countries within the Union were given leeway in imports and exports; however there was a tariff in place for countries outside of the Community. De Gaulle won in getting the tariff in place, while the other nations were forced to accept it or leave the Community. Furthermore, Delors and De Gaulle's visions of a European Federation were not implanted. The European Community became a gathering of sovereign nations seeking to grow and prosper socially, politically, and economically. The words of Thatcher and Monnet succeeded in preserving nationalistic pride and independence. In respect to the involvement with external nations, such as the United States and Great Britain, the European Union chose to open itself up to globalization. Great Britain became a member of the European Community, while the Community chose to strengthen its relationship with the United States for defense and economic purposes. The visions of Thatcher, De Gaulle, Monnet, and Delors were realized in parts because each member made strong contributions to the overall success of Europe and its needs for the future.

Stress during WWII

Mere decades after the end of World War I, the men of Europe found themselves trudging along the front lines of World War II. WWII was a war that Europe could not have prepared its men to endure, yet nonetheless they were forced to do so. As Nazi Germany drew in the concern of Britain, Poland, France, and Russia, the entire world witnessed the deteriorating fabrics of Europe, as well as the morale of its people. One might ask, how did the soldiers, behind both lines, manage to deal with the stresses of the war? Three accounts of soldiers in World War II successfully highlight the physical and abstract notions/outlets that were used by the soldiers to remain sturdy throughout the war. Richard Holmes's *The Italian Job: Five Armies in Italy, 1943-1945*, Gottlob Hebert Bidermann's *In Deadly Combat: A German Soldier's Memoir of the Eastern Front*, and Antony Beever's and Luba Vinogradova's *A Writer at War: Vasily Grossman with the Red Army* provide examples of ways that soldiers dealt with the stresses of war. Throughout World War II, the soldiers dealt with the stresses of war by attributing their purpose to nationalism, by maintaining strong camaraderie, and through the small tokens of recreation that reminded the soldiers of a better time.

World War II left soldiers fearing for their lives as they avoided the dangers of the front lines, thus the soldiers' abilities to regard their purpose in the war as nationalism aided in relieving the stresses of the war. Nationalism relieves these stresses in two ways: the receiving of medals and nationalistic pride. First, a common symbol allows the soldiers to feel recognized for contributing to their nation was medals. For example, in Beever's *A Writer at War*, a soldier fighting under Kozlov mentions that "Kozlov gave me a medal" and that a soldier he admired "received two medals that morning" (Beevor, 104). In both situations, the medals were handed out without ceremony (one taken off another dead soldier) and given to the soldiers to relieve them of the stresses of the war. The soldier discusses the receipt of the medal as his nation recognizing the duties that he is fulfilling for the sake of his nation. This medal gives him the power to fight further in the war. Moreover, the soldier accounts in *In Deadly Combat* show that the soldiers revered other soldiers who were awarded with medals. The medals symbolized the soldiers' dedication to their nation. Bidermann writes, from the perspective of a soldier, "The battalion commander . . . had accomplished this feat only through the use of his extraordinary leadership skills . . . [he was] awarded the Knight's Cross of the Iron Cross" (Bidermann, 148). In both instances, the soldiers cling to those medals as a reason to fight, regardless of the dangers. They feel appreciation knowing that they are doing their nation a service.

      In addition to the medals taking pressure off the men, the soldiers dealt with the stresses of war through feelings of nationalistic pride. For example, in *A Writer at War*, Beevor writes, "[according to Grossman on Russian soldiers] He may live in sin, but he dies a saint," implying that Russian soldiers go into the war scared but they die for their nation (Beevor, 95). This allows them to be focused and fight in the war with a sense of nationalistic entitlement. Moreover, a German Commisar told retreating soldiers, "Go forward, for our Motherland," which inspired the fearful soldiers to brave the battlefield for their homeland (102). The soldiers used nationalistic pride to forgo the stress that war impends on the soldier's body and soul. This appears in *The Italian Job*, also. In regards to the German Army, Holmes recounts two German officers who "radiated 'pride in his country and his men'" (Holmes, 213). Holmes states that the German Army was "bound together by nationalism," which is instilled in the soldierly virtues (213). The German soldiers are taught to replace stress with nationalistic pride. Lastly, an Englishwoman stated, "But there is not one of them [German soldiers] who does not express his blind conviction that Germany cannot be beaten," even though they had lost the war (213). Each statement provided insight to the mindset that soldiers used to avoid the stresses of war and justify the strain of conflict.

Brotherhood and camaraderie were the main outlets for the soldiers to deal with the ongoing pressures of the war. As World War II stripped soldiers of a normal life, thrusting them into strange lands with strangers, the men found comfort in the familial-like relationships that formed within army divisions. For example, in *The Italian Job* the author comments that "The fellows don't want to leave when they're sick. They're afraid to leave their own men—the men they know. It gives you more guts to be with them" (210). Holmes goes on to say, "it was a family business [that gave you] an inner confidence and belonging" (211). Furthermore, in *In Deadly Combat*, the bond was so strong that soldiers sought out revenge when fellow men fell to the hand of the enemy: "Destroy the attackers, kill them, those who have destroyed those close to you" (Bidermann, 263). The camaraderie with the fellow soldiers became more personal than a work relationship. These men were able to rely on each other. They could be themselves within a realm that did not recognize individualism. The brotherhood strengthened soldiers' abilities to continue to fight. It preserved these men from falling under the perils of the war, allowing them to fight for their cause.

    Moreover, soldiers put the strains of war aside through small tokens of joy that reminded them of their former civilian lives. First, the arena of war was depressing, but the men put this depression aside by enjoying the use of song. For example, a motorized infantry battalion solider was quoted in *A Writer at War*, "But now is the best time to sing songs," claiming that singing songs from his home country diverted his attention from the traumas of war (Beevor, 105). In the same light, a solider was quoted saying, "it's good if there's an amusing fellow, who starts to tell or sing something funny," concerning what takes his mind off the war (107). On a sadder note, a soldier stated, "the faint sound of 'Silent Night, Holy Night' could be detected" after a large conflict had occurred between enemies (Bidermann, 266). The soldiers sung even after a major loss occurred. Clearly, the use of song allowed the men to feel at ease in a time of great risk. Along with song, the soldiers relied heavily on food to comfort them during the war. The German soldiers of *In Deadly Combat* consistently refer to the food that they were eating with great detail during the breaks between gunfire. One battalion said, "we boiled freshly dug potatoes . . . plucked a chicken, [and] we ate peeled cucumbers" and, "the kitchen sent forward hot coffee and schmalzbrot" (24 and 25). The culturally driven food, plus the feeling of a warm meal, gave them the strength to push forward and forget the war for a moment. Moreover, Bidermann noted a hard-working priest who "was constantly on the move with his worn field pack strapped to his back [providing] the troops with simple food items," which were luxuries to the men during hard gunfire (149). The food provided the men with sweet reminders of home that relieved them of the anxieties caused by the hardship of war. In every instance noted, the men behaved as if they were not at war when they were savoring meals that took their minds away from the war at hand.

    As with all wars, it can take a serious toll on the emotional psyche and the physical well-being of the soldiers on the front lines. During World War II, these soldiers bore witness to the harshest environments and ugliest battlefields know to Europe's history. The men were forced to witness the gruesome deaths of fellow men, asked to forget their civilian life, and expected to be willing to die for a cause larger than they could grasp. Although the war placed a tremendous amount of stress on the soldiers, they managed to siphon hope and comfort in fighting the war for the motherland, singing songs, savoring comfort foods, and forming ironclad bonds with their fellow soldiers. By convincing them that they were fighting to protect their nation, it instilled nationalistic pride that allowed them to overlook the dying men around them and continue to fight. The seemingly worthless medals pried off dead soldiers' bodies and awarded to others gave them that sense of accomplishment; it told them they there were succeeding, and each step took them closer to victory. Additionally, the food stopped the war, giving these soldiers a short, but much needed, reprieve from the terrors of World War II. Lastly, the relationship known as brotherhood, gave these men the strength to move forward. These small tokens of life preserved the men during the war allowing them to fight with pride and die with dignity. It made them fearless. It gave them resources for coping. Without these resources, the soldiers who fought in World War II would have failed to trudge into combat.

As a Whole: The Intersection of Brooks and Moretti

Literature is a glimpse of the sociopolitical environment of an era. It tells a story. It provides a platform for theorists to unravel. More importantly, literature follows specific constructs, conveys certain meanings, and is an experience. Two common theories, close-reading and distant-reading evaluate literature at distinct levels with close reading peering into the structure and content of prose/poetry and distant reading examining the impacts of society on literature (and vice versa). Cleanth Brooks, a well-known close-reading theorist, establishes his theory in the essay "The Well Wrought Urn," which focuses on understanding the poem as a whole, explaining that a poem cannot be deconstructed into fragments and that a reader must not paraphrase a poem, as it damages the poem's original intent. Secondly, Franco Moretti, a distant reader, developed a theory far from the realm of Brooks in "Graphs, Maps and Trees:

Abstract Models for a Literary History," an essay that proclaims that literature can be understood when viewed from afar. These theories, while very different, with Brooks criticizing the structure and unity of poetry and Moretti evaluating the cultural impact on novel genres and their unity, both focus on patterns, structure, and unity. The approaches are logical whilst maintaining a literary perspective; this common denominator is more important than the dissimilarities among their theories. The literary theories of Brooks and Moretti are strikingly different, however both theorists choose a logical approach to analyze literature at the level of the poem (Brooks) or at the level of all novels (Moretti) in which both theorists examine literature as a whole rather than subjecting it to a deconstructed meaning generated by its readers.

    The close-reading theory established by Brooks and the distant-reading theory illustrated by Moretti both agree that literature is best understood as a unit that should not be dismantled for meaning. According to Brooks, literature at the level of the poem should be read and understood without having to analyze the fragments (i.e. sentences or words). For example, Brooks states that "we must draw a sharp distinction between the attractiveness or beauty of any particular item taken as such and the 'beauty' of the poem considered as a whole" (1218). Thus, the reader should not evaluate the words and sentences of the poem on their own, but the poem should be read as a whole to gather the core meaning (1218). Even further, paraphrasing the poem instead of reading it in its original form would strip the poem of its inherent meaning, as "form and content, or content and medium are inseparable" from the truth of the poem (1221). Much like Brooks, Moretti strongly suggests that literature be examined as a whole, rather than selecting a few dozen novels to generalize the sum of the novel genre. He states that the novel "cannot be understood by stitching together separate bits of knowledge about individual cases, because it isn't a sum of individual cases: it's a collective system" and "should be grasped as a whole" (2442). Selecting a handful of novels does not give an accurate account of what literature is or what defines it, which is why Moretti makes this claim. He throws the canon into the abyss and takes a logical approach to evaluate the entire production of all novels throughout history. Moretti indicates that literature can only be understood if "we [must] explain the pattern as a whole" (2449). Thus, watching the trends of novels throughout history will give a truer sense to the meaning of novels during the eras in which they are written. Although Brooks and Moretti do not agree about the depth in which literature should be analyzed, both critics cite that literature be evaluated as a unit that follows patterns and structures. Only when a reader can experience the poem as a poem or grasp that all novels contribute to culture (and vice versa), will the academy be able to interpret the inherent truths that lie within literature.

    In addition to examining poems and novels as units, Brooks and Moretti express the need to read poems and novels without subjecting them to one's own personal emotions, therefore preserving the poetry and novels as units of art. This keeps the critical analysis as a logical one that leaves the literature free from misinterpretation. First, Brooks is an advocate for keeping external perspectives outside of the structure and form of the poem that author penned for a specific purpose. Reading a poem is an experience, but it is not "a mere statement about experience," thus the poem is a part of life, not a medium in which the reader is to take something away from it (1228). This leads into the logical approach to close reading poetry that Brooks discusses in this essay; he believes that "poetry . . . makes no use of ideas, or that either is merely emotional" (1228). He is saying that the truth of a poem—the truth that the author wrote into its words, structure and form— are separate from those emotions or former experiences that the reader may have and therefore those emotions must be external to the literary analysis. Moretti mirrors this ideology in his theory as well, and commands that literature be analyzed from a scientific and logical perspective. Dissecting novels teaches nothing of the purpose and meaning of literature, thus quantitative analysis of the novel genre will yield the core meaning of literature (2445). Moretti goes on to say that a quantitative approach of the genre as a whole "is ideally independent of interpretations" that leads to an objective interpretation of novels, rather than a subjective one (2445). The two theorists are synchronous in preserving the "essence" of literature and both declare that as scholars, we should not search for "the general effect" of literature (the paraphrase of a poem or analysis of a novel, which is convoluted with personal projections), rather the academy must strip away the subjective analysis for an objective analysis that exposes "the real core meaning" of the art as a "collective system" (1219 and 2442).

    This logical and collective approach to literature is more important than the other components of each literary theory. As Brooks and Moretti agree on unity and objective analysis, they do not agree on a canon and the depth of the reading, however these two components of each theory do not compare to the theorists' desire to have literature critically analyzed through a specific method. Analyzing literature as a whole rather than choosing to select or not to select a canon will strengthen the academy's grasp on the depth and sociopolitical implications of novels and poetry. Brooks advocates a narrow canon of a dozen poems that he feels sum up the excellent literature (in poetry) of history, while Moretti suggests not reading any novels at all, as it would not result in a collective analysis of the novel genre. Brooks narrow canon does not provide an insight into the meaning of literature. However, his objective method of analysis, choosing not to break apart the poem into fragments and to "preserve the unity" of poetry makes his theory one to be commended (1229). Keeping a poem whole exemplifies the authorial intent of the poem, illustrates the "straightforward formulation," and extracts the meaning of it as a "rational statement" of art (1227). It avoids invading the words, structure, and form from personal experience. On the other side, distant reading, as expressed by Moretti has no canon from which the academy reads. In fact, he suggests not reading at all, exclaiming that it is the historical data of book history that provides the academy the sociopolitical meaning that literature lends to culture (2442 and 2462). Not reading literature seems absurd, but he makes a viable stance, as this method strips the process from any external bias because he is analyzing the trends of all novels throughout history and interpreting it as the impact of culture on writing and the impact of writing on culture. Gaining a clearer understanding of the implications of literature throughout the ages is more important than selecting a canon or reading anything for that matter. Brooks and Moretti do not have to agree on a canon, as they both agree that their field of literature would do much better without "emphasizing the uniqueness" of individual words or individual novels (2441). The theorists want to examine it in unity and extract its natural truth; this ideology is critical to the academy and trumps the notion of canons and the exact depth of the reading. Adapting a logical and less subjective method for literary analysis will rid the English department of loaded ideals and bring the department to a unified understanding of the importance of novels and poetry with respect to authorial intent, structure, form, and the sociopolitical purpose of literature as a whole.

Theory in literature can put the Department of English in muddy water. There are critics who believe in close reading, there are critics who read from afar, and there are critics who find themselves stuck in the middle. Oftentimes, close and distant theories are in opposition, much like Brooks and Moretti, yet there are intersections within these theories in which the theorists can stand together. Moretti and Brooks have that intersection in a most important aspect: they both fight for an objective analysis of all literature that evaluates the inherent truths and implications of poetry and novels as a whole. While Moretti examines all novels and Brooks views individual poems (a component on which they definitely disagree), the men do not separate the words and impress an individualized meaning to the medium/content. Brooks examines the whole of a poem as it is melted together with its structure and form; he says that the poem is an experience that cannot be turned into altering experiences for each reader. In relation to this, Moretti compiles vast amounts of literary data on novel trends, then abstracts the meaning and importance of novels throughout history. He does not separate the novels into eras or sections—he criticizes novels as a whole. The theorists attempt to make a logical, even scientific approach to literature, which is an approach that would serve the academy well. Perhaps these theories could be melted together to give birth to a theory that abstracts sociopolitical influence, an objective method of analysis, and a well-balanced style of literary criticism.

Six Degrees of Thingness: Or Just a Pun on Words.

Does anything matter? Or is everything a social construction that can be deconstructed in critical theory? There is much conversation of such notions going on in the classroom; the topic of LaTour's objectivity provides a noteworthy perspective to objects containing thingness in the past theories read in this course. To make for a coherent argument, a Thing is not an object sitting on a table; rather it commands a gathering. It is both thing and the societies that convene at the Thing. Eroding deconstruction and claiming that reality need not be subjected to the perils of criticism is LaTour's cornerstone. The ideologies behind literature, politics, and technology are within the objects that become things the moment that they receive a monumental of attention. Things are handcrafted, while objects are manufactured. Two theorists have presented objects appreciated for its thingness in a manner that avoids the negative criticism that LaTour exploits in *Why Has Critique Run Out of Steam* providing an excellent platform for objectivity. In Cleanth Brooks's *The Well Wrought Urn*, he presents the poem as a Thing. On the other hand, Jodi Dean pens technological theory on blogs in *Blog Theory: Feedback and Capture in the Circuits of Drive*, where she presents the importance of the blog as a means for communication. Likewise, the critics show Things that command different gatherings, leading one to ask, 'why is one matter of concern different than the other?' To answer this question, we will examine the degrees of "thingness" given to a Thing and the gatherings that convene at the thing. Brooks's poem and Dean's blog present objects with degrees of "thingness" that avoid some threats of negative criticism mentioned in LaTour's essay on objectivity; the difference between poetry and the blog as Things are the gatherings and the events that lead to their rise and fall of importance in the eyes of those within the gathering.

In each essay, an object has degrees of "thingness" that command different gatherings and carry different matters of concern. For Brooks, his object that has "Thingness" is the poem. A poem is a structure that takes intangible ideas (e.g. love, politics, and religion) and turns them into tangible words on the paper. According to Brooks, the poem is a medium that is an experience not created for one to subject it to further interpretation (1218). Furthermore, the poem is a handcrafted piece of expression that is filled with ideologies addressing an issue, which is the very definition of a Thing, according to LaTour (2288). A poem is a Thing because it commands a gathering interested in its purpose. An important gathering of the poem is the gathering that requires the poem to fulfill an obligation. First, the gathering that requires the poem to fulfill an obligation, turns a poem from an object into a Thing within moments and then allows it to be objectified again. For example, if a class requires that students to read Edgar Allen Poe's "The Raven," then the poem will become a Thing as its relevance impacts the students' success (2290). The object rises and falls from "Thingness" as it fulfills the gatherings needs (2292). Moreover, the poem may retain Thingness if the reader interprets the lines of poetry in relation to his/her life, thereby it becomes a representation of more than words to gain achievement or to represent literature; it forges a personal understanding (1228). It may become a Thing long after it is no longer "needed," but with a newfound Thingness.

Additionally, the blog in Dean's excerpt "The Death of Blogging" qualifies as a Thing because it is handcrafted and has several gatherings. The blog represents ideas in a technological aspect that captivates several gatherings. According to Dean, the blog is not a platform for the blogger to write about anything, but it is an "illusion of a core, true, essential, and singular self" that represents one's feelings of interconnectedness with society (Dean, 56). The blog allows the writer to express ideas or connect socially with others. It becomes a Thing when many bloggers gather in the "Blogipelago" to communicate with one another (Dean, 46). This communication tool turns from object to Thing when its bloggers transform blogging into "a relationship," and the "features of the blog . . . contribute to cross-blog connections and conversations" (Dean, 44). It turns from manufactured technology to a synthetic medium for which social relationships can be born.

     Blog gatherings include the individual blogger and the readers of the blog. Gatherings of blogs are specific to content and may fluctuate if the blog fails to maintain the gathering's interest (Dean, 56). A blog serves as the freedom of expression of the blogger, who becomes its sole audience. The blogger is the gathering, as LaTour cites that it is not the number of the gathering that gives an object Thingness, but it is the stability of that gathering to maintain its interest in the object (2300). The individual posts her opinions on life or society, which, to the blogger, are matters of concern. The second gathering of the blog is the bloggers commenting on the blog and connecting with the blogger. The gathering is captivated if the blog maintains posts and is interesting, yet the blog can have degrees of Thingness (Dean, 47). For example, Dean mentions that in the birth of the blog, millions convened in the Blogosphere, however blogs became less popular. This is the case in which the object becomes a Thing and then turns back into an object (not permanently, it can always be re-thingified) (2291). The blog much like the poem have moments of thingness, moments of objecthood, and gatherings that maintain the cycle.

The poem and blog are things, but how do we tell the difference between them? Each thing bears importance to its society, yet they stand for different ideologies that lure gatherings to its Thingness. We can tell the difference between these Things and their gatherings by evaluating what they are, the degrees of Thingness and the types of gatherings involved. First, Dean's blog is a technological platform for communication between bloggers and readers. It is one's ability to express opinions without conforming to a standard. It creates relationships without attachments (Dean, 44). Alternatively, the poem in Brooks's essay is a written form of art that turns the intangible into tangible forms (1228). It represents an individual's ability to relate to social ideology and it demonstrates high quality standards to those learning about literature. The blog speaks to the citizen of everyday vernacular, while the poem speaks to the academics. Secondly, both Things have varying degrees of Thingness throughout its history in society. The blog, unlike the poem, experiences more variance in the amount of Thingness that it contains, thereby gaining and losing its gathering every now and again. For instance, a well-known poem becomes a Thing perpetually to the Department of English and it is revered for its contribution to literature. It may lose a bit of its Thingness if a newer, more sophisticated poem enters the stage, but it will always have Thingness. However, this poem may be objectified by the students forced to turn it into a Thing once they are no longer required to treat the poem as a Thing (2292). Unlike the poem, the blog's Thingness and its gathering change more quickly than the poem. For example, during the height of a blog's popularity, the gathering is stronger and its Thingness is represented in the importance of the information to the gathering. As more blogs surface, the gathering will adapt to include those who are interested in the blog topic. Relationships are formed between the blogger and the readers. It may lose Thingness if the blogger stops posting to the blog, as well. Conversely, the blog, as we can see with the birth of Twitter and Facebook, will lose its Thingness (if it has not already) and revert to an object as new social media dominate the internet (Dean, 35). We can tell the difference between the poem and the blog because the poem maintains its Thingness more so than the blog. Moreover, we can tell the difference between the gatherings of the poem and the blog: the poem is viewed by the academic arena, while the gatherings of a blog are interested in the topic or the desire to communicate with others.

    The difference between the Things and the gatherings matter, otherwise everything would have equal bearing. A frivolous tweet does not stand on the same level as a poem earning a Pulitzer. According to Brooks, the poem is an experience that does not warrant a dialogue between its substance and its reader (1227). A stellar poem will remain a Thing for all because it has the ability to connect with its gathering. Its gathering seeks to solve problems with the poems solution and is not intended for a frivolous analysis. Additionally, the blog is something that anybody can write, that anybody can read, and most importantly, that anybody can forgo in an instant. These factors make the difference between high quality writing and everyday technological vernacular matter.

    According to LaTour, fetishism and unconscious factors are forms of criticism used to explain the representation of Thingness within an object. Both the blog and the poem encounter and evade these criticisms used to debunk the "thingness" of Things. The first criticism regarding fetish claims "the object is simply a projection of their [readers'] wishes onto a material entity that does nothing at all by itself" (2292). While some may choose to read a poem because they feel that they relate to it, Brooks is clear to state that a poem is an experience, however it is not an object which one can subjectively interpret for one's own (1228). The poem avoids such pitfalls of critics attempting to deconstruct the poem for qualities less than it deserves, as the poem can stand all by itself. Similarly, the blog seems to succumb to the fetishizing criticism, even Dean claims that "[the blog] is parasitic, narcissistic, and pointless" as it is a projected reality that puts the self on a stage for others to see and form cyber relationships with (Dean, 37). However, Dean points out that this feeling of self-worth and popularity is what gives the blog its Thingness and this is not a fetish-made object. The blog and the poem avoid the second form of criticism, as well. The second form of criticism, according to LaTour, is claiming that the people giving Thingness to these objects do not know that their reactions or behaviors are the product of subconscious factors such as drive, interests, and genetics (2294). This is harder to fight against for each Thing, but it is clear that the poem avoids these perils whilst the blog succumbs to it. According to Dean, drive and desire fuel the blog. She claims that readers hunger for new posts and the blogger is driven to feed such a hunger, whether, they know that they are feeding the reader (Dean, 43). Here, the blog, in all its

Thingness, does fall to the criticism that it is a Thing because it motivates and satiates drives that are underlying the conscious.

Objectivity and Thingness can make everything that we as critics fall apart. The teddy bear that a child hugs is more than a teddy bear; it symbolizes comfort and love, at least while the gathering feels so. LaTour exploits the notion that an object can become a thing as quickly as it transforms back into an object. Poetry in Brooks's *The Well Wrought Urn* and the blog in Dean's "The Death of Blogging" are objects that have been Thingified. Each Thing has experienced degrees of Thingness, which hinge in the gathering, as well as its ability to maintain the gathering. Both Things face the criticism of literary scholars and are subjected to the notion that they may just be objects that have been projected upon. Perhaps this is true for some, but for the most part, the poem and the blog stand on their own. They are Things which command a gathering because what their Thingness is, is enough to avoid such criticisms.

Works Cited

Addison, Paul and Angus Calder. *Experience of War in the West, 1939-1945.* . London: Pimlico, 1997. Print.

Alger, Horatio. *Alger, Horatio. Ragged Dick, Or, Street Life in New York with the Boot-blacks*. New York: Modern Library, 2005. Print.

Alulis, Joseph. "Wisdom and Fortune: The Education of the Prince in Shakespeare's King Lear." *Interpretation* 20.3 (1994): 373-390. Web.

Beardsworth, Adam. "The Poetics of Double-talk: John Berryman's Dream Songs as Cold War Testimonials." *Exegesis* (n.d.): 32-40. Print.

Beevor, Antony and Luba Vinogradova. " A Writer at War: Vasily Grossman with the Red Army, 1941- 1945." New York: Pantheon, 2005. Print.

Bernstein, Charles. *Recalculating*. n.d.

Berryman, John. *The Dream Songs*. New York: Farrar, Straus and Giroux, 1969. Print.

Berssenbrugge, Mei-Mei. "The New Boys." *Hello, the Roses*. n.d.

Bidermann, G. H., G.H. and Derek S Zumbro. "In Deadly Combat: A German Soldier's Memoir of the Eastern Front." University of Kansas, 2000. Print.

Biscoglio, Frances. "Invocations to the Gods in King Lear." *Shakespeare Newsletter*. n.d.

Blundell, Sue. *Women in Ancient Greece*. Harvard: Cambridge, 1995. Print.

Brooks, Cleanth. "The Well Wrought Urn." (n.d.).

Brooks, Gwendolyn. "The Mother." n.d.

Cohen, David. *Law, Sexuality, and Society: The Enforcement of Morals in Classical Athens*. Cambridge : Cambridge UP, 1991. Print.

—. "Seclusion, Separation, and the Status of Women in Classical Athens." *Greece and Rome* 1987.1 (1987): 3-15.

Conrad, CA. "How the Fuck Do I Get Out of this Place." Conrad, CA.

Ecodeviance. Wave Books, n.d. Print.

Couch, Ben. "The No-Man's-Land Of "A New England Nun"." *Studies in Short Fiction* (1998): 187. Print.

Creasy, Jonathan. "Susan Howe's Telepathy "." *The Los Angeles Review of Books.* 20 January 2015: 1-15. Print.

Crown, Kathleen. ""This Unstable L-witnessing": Susan Howe's Lyric Iconoclasm and the Articulating Ghost." *Women's Studies: An Interdisciplinary Journal* (2010).

Daniels, Anthony. "Diagnosing Lear." *The New Criterion* (2007).

Danticat, Edwidge. *Breath, Eyes, Memory*. Vintage , 1998. Print.

Dean, Jodi. *Blog Theory: Feedback and Capture in the Circuits of Drive* . n.d.

Delors, Jacques. "A Necessary Union." n.d.

Deming, Richard. "Out of Reach." *The Boston Review* 11 May 2011. Print.

Descartes, René. *Discourse on Method ; And, Meditations on First Philosophy*. Ed. Donald A. Cress. Indianapolis: Hackett , 1998. Print.

Dilbeck, Keiko. "Symbolic Representation of Identity In Hurston's Their Eyes Were Watching God." *Explicator* (2008): 102-104. Print.

Dimovitz, Scott. "I Was the Subject Sentence Written on the Mirror: Angela Carter's Short Fiction and the Unwriting of the Psychoanalytic Subject ." *Literature Interpretation Theory* (2012): 1-19. Web.

Eliot, T.S. *The Wasteland*. n.d.

Freeman, Mary W. "A New England Nun ." *The Heath Anthology of American Literature*. Fifth. Vol. C. Boston: Houghton Mifflin, 2006. 715-723. Print.

Garry, Ann. "Intersectionality, Metaphors, And The Multiplicity Of Gender." *Hypatia* 26.4 (2011): 826-850. Web.

Gaulle, Charles de. "Europe." n.d.

Gray, Thomas. "Elegy Written in a Country Churchyard." n.d.

Heaney, Seamus. "198. Bog Queen." *OPENED GROUND*. Farrar, Straus and Giroux, 1999. Print.

Herack, Katrina. "Representing Alterity: The Temporal Aesthetics of Susan

Howe and Charles Olson." *Canadian Review of American Studies* 43.3 (2013). Web.

Holmes, Richard. *Time to kill : the soldier's experience of war in the West, 1939-1945*. London: Pimlico, 1997. Print.

Howe, Susan. *That This*. New York: New Directions, 2010. Print.

Hurston, Zora Neale. *Their Eyes Were Watching God*. New York: Perennial Library, n.d.

Kane, Sarah. n.d. Print.

Katz, Marilyn. "Ideology and "The Status of Women" in Ancient Greece." *History and Theory* (1992): 70-97. Web.

Kubitschek, Missy D. "Tuh De Horizon and Back": The Female Quest in Their Eyes Were Watching God." *Black American Literature Forum* (1983): 109-115. Web.

Kuhlman, Alyssa. "The Foil of Fosdick." (n.d.): 1-4. Print.

Lau, K.J. "Erotic infidelities: Angela carter's wolf trilogy." *Marvels & Tales: Journal of Fairy-Tale Studies* 22.1 (2008): 77-94. Print.

Markman, Alan M. "The Meaning of "Sir Gawain and the Green Knight"." *PMLA* 72.4 (1957): 574-586. Web. <http://www.jstor.org/stable/460169>.

McLane, Maureen. "The Paris Review." *Paris Review* (2012). Web.

Monnet, Jean. "A Ferment for Change." n.d.

Montaigne, Michel De. *On Experience. Essays*. Ed. J.M. Cohen. Baltimore: Penguin, 1970. Print.

Moretti, Franco. "Graphs, Maps and Trees: Abstract Models for a Literary History." (n.d.).

Mullen, Harryette. *S*p*rm**k*t*. n.d.

Nicholls, Peter. "The Pastness of Landscape": Susan Howe's "Pierce-Arrow"." *Contemporary Literature* (2002): 441-460. Print.

Podnieks, Elizabeth. "Maternal Literatures in Text and Tradition: Daughter-Centric, Matrilineal, and Matrifocal Perspectives." n.d.

Porter, Dorothy. "The Heroic Age: The Social Centrality of Women in Beowulf." Western Michigan University, 2002. Print.

Rankine, Claudia. *Citizen*. n.d.

Rex, Cathy. ""Mixed-Blood" Womanhood: Pocahontas, The Female American, and Feminine Authorial." Rex, Cathy. *INDIANNESS AND WOMANHOOD: TEXTUALIZING THE FEMALE*. Auburn: UMI Dissertation Publishing, 2008. 221-300. Print.

Rowson, Susanna. *Charlotte Temple*. Boston: Bedford-St. Martin's, 2011. Print.

Schanoes, Veronica. "Fearless Children and Fabulous Monsters: Angela Carter, Lewis Carroll, and Beastly Girls." *" Marvels & Tales* 26.1 (2012): 30-44. Web. <http://muse.jhu.edu/>.

Semonovitch, Kascha. "Life, Lines: Susan Howe's That This and Julie Carr's Sarah-Of Fragments and Lines." *Kenyon Review Winter* (2012). Web.

Settles, Isis H. "Use of an Intersectional Framework to Understand Black Women's Racial and Gender Identities." *Sex Roles* (2006): 589-601. Web.

Shakespeare, William. "King Lear ." Greenblatt, Stephen. *The Norton Anthology of English Literature*. New York: W.W. Norton, 2006. 1143-1227. Print.

Sherry, James. "Pride and Prejudice: The Limits of Society." *Studies in English Literature, 1500-1900* 19.4 (1979): 609-622. Web. 2013. <http://www.jstor.org/stable/450251>.

Simmons, Ryan. "The Hierarchy Itself': Hurston's Their Eyes Were Watching God and the Sacrifice of Narrative Authority." *African American Review* (2002): 181-193. Web.

"Sir Gawain and the Green Knight." Lawall, Sarah N. *The Norton Anthology of World Literature*. Ed. Maynard Mack. 2. New York: Norton, 2001. 1991-2045. Print.

Smith, Nicole. "Representations of Women in Medieval Literature: Margery Kempe, Gawain, and Beowulf." *Article Myriad* (2008). Print.

Spinoza, Benedictus De. *Theological-political Treatise*. Cambridge: Cambridge, 2007. Print.

Swensen, Cole. "Sometimes the Ghost." *Gravesend*. n.d.

Thatcher, Margaret. "Speech to the College of Europe, Bruges, ." 1988.

Unknown. *Beowulf*. Ed. John McNamara and George Stade. New York: Barnes & Noble Classics, 2005.

West, Christompher A. "Candles Lighting the Dark': The Birth-mark's Antinomian Method." *Textual Practice* (2013). Web.

Whitman, Walt. "Out of the Cradle Endlessly Rocking." *Leaves of Grass*. 1860.

Winkfield, Unca Eliza. *The Female American, Or, The Adventures of Unca Eliza Winkfield*. Ontario: Broadview, 2001. Print.

Wordsworth, William. "Nutting." *The Complete Poetical Works of William Wordsworth*. Cosimo Classics, 2008. Print.

Xenophon. "Husbands, Wives and the Household Oeconomicus." *Oeconomicus VII* (n.d.). Print.

www.ingramcontent.com/pod-product-compliance
Lightning Source LLC
Chambersburg PA
CBHW021428080526
44588CB00009B/461